THE SHIFT

D1630778

**Other Hay House Products
by Dr. Wayne W. Dyer**

<u>BOOKS</u>

Being in Balance
Change Your Thoughts—Change Your Life
Everyday Wisdom
Everyday Wisdom for Success
Excuses Begone!
Getting in the Gap (book-with-CD)
Incredible You! (children's book with Kristina Tracy)
Inspiration
The Invisible Force
It's Not What You've Got! (children's book with Kristina
Tracy)
Living the Wisdom of the Tao
No Excuses! (children's book with Kristina Tracy)
The Power of Intention
The Power of Intention gift edition (available October
2010)
A Promise Is a Promise
Staying on the Path
10 Secrets for Success and Inner Peace

Unstoppable Me! (children's book with Kristina Tracy)
Your Ultimate Calling

<u>AUDIO/CD PROGRAMS</u>

Advancing Your Spirit (with Marianne Williamson)
Applying the 10 Secrets for Success and Inner Peace
The Caroline Myss & Wayne Dyer Seminar
Change Your Thoughts—Change Your Life
(unabridged audio book)
Change Your Thoughts Meditation

Everyday Wisdom (audio book)
Excuses Begone! (available as an audio book and a lecture)
How to Get What You Really, Really, Really, Really Want
Inspiration (abridged 4-CD set)
Inspirational Thoughts
Making Your Thoughts Work for You (with Byron Katie)
Meditations for Manifesting
101 Ways to Transform Your Life (audio book)
The Power of Intention (abridged 4-CD set)
A Promise Is a Promise (audio book)
The Secrets of the Power of Intention (6-CD set)
10 Secrets for Success and Inner Peace
There Is a Spiritual Solution to Every Problem
The Wayne Dyer Audio Collection/CD Collection
Your Journey to Enlightenment (6-tape program)

DVDs

Change Your Thoughts—Change Your Life
Excuses Begone!
Inspiration
The Power of Intention
The Shift, the movie (available as a 1-DVD
program and an expanded 2-DVD set)
10 Secrets for Success and Inner Peace

There's a Spiritual Solution to Every Problem

MISCELLANEOUS

Change Your Thoughts—Change Your Life
Perpetual Flip Calendar
Everyday Wisdom Perpetual Flip Calendar
Inner Peace Cards
Inspiration Cards
Inspiration Perpetual Flip Calendar
The Power of Intention Cards

The Power of Intention Perpetual Flip Calendar
The Shift Box Set (includes *The Shift* DVD and
The Shift tradepaper book)
10 Secrets for Success and Inner Peace Cards
10 Secrets for Success and Inner Peace gift products:
<u>*Notecards, Candle,*</u> and <u>*Journal*</u>

All of the above are available at your local bookstore,
or may be ordered by visiting:

Hay House UK: **www.hayhouse.co.uk**
Hay House USA: **www.hayhouse.com**
Hay House Australia: **www.hayhouse.com.au**
Hay House South Africa: **www.hayhouse.co.za**
Hay House India: **www.hayhouse.co.in**

"There is a land of the living and a land of the dead and the bridge is love, the only survival, the only meaning."

— from *The Bridge of San Luis Rey,*
by Thornton Wilder

THE SHIFT

Taking *Your* Life From Ambition to Meaning

Dr Wayne W. Dyer

HAY HOUSE

Australia • Canada • Hong Kong • India
South Africa • United Kingdom • United States

First published and distributed in the United Kingdom by:
Hay House UK Ltd, 292B Kensal Rd, London W10 5BE. Tel.: (44) 20 8962 1230;
Fax: (44) 20 8962 1239. www.hayhouse.co.uk

Published and distributed in the United States of America by:
Hay House, Inc., PO Box 5100, Carlsbad, CA 92018-5100. Tel.: (1) 760 431 7695
or (800) 654 5126; Fax: (1) 760 431 6948 or (800) 650 5115. www.hayhouse.com

Published and distributed in Australia by:
Hay House Australia Ltd, 18/36 Ralph St, Alexandria NSW 2015. Tel.: (61) 2 9669
4299; Fax: (61) 2 9669 4144. www.hayhouse.com.au

Published and distributed in the Republic of South Africa by:
Hay House SA (Pty), Ltd, PO Box 990, Witkoppen 2068. Tel./Fax: (27) 11 467
8904. www.hayhouse.co.za

Published and distributed in India by:
Hay House Publishers India, Muskaan Complex, Plot No.3, B-2, Vasant Kunj,
New Delhi – 110 070. Tel.: (91) 11 4176 1620; Fax: (91) 11 4176 1630.
www.hayhouse.co.in

Distributed in Canada by:
Raincoast, 9050 Shaughnessy St, Vancouver, BC V6P 6E5. Tel.: (1) 604 323 7100;
Fax: (1) 604 323 2600

Copyright © 2010 by Wayne W. Dyer

Editorial supervision: Jill Kramer • *Wayne Dyer's editor:* Joanna Pyle
Project editor: Shannon Littrell • *Design:* Riann Bender

The moral rights of the author have been asserted.

The author of this book does not dispense medical advice or prescribe the use of
any technique as a form of treatment for physical or medical problems without
the advice of a physician, either directly or indirectly. The intent of the author
is only to offer information of a general nature to help you in your quest for
emotional and spiritual wellbeing. In the event you use any of the information
in this book for yourself, which is your constitutional right, the author and the
publisher assume no responsibility for your actions.

A catalogue record for this book is available from the British Library.

ISBN 978-1-8485-0041-9

Printed and bound in Great Britain by CPI Bookmarque, Croydon, CR0 4TD.

For Reid Tracy.
I'm so grateful that we shared this vision together. . . .

C O N T E N T S

INTRODUCTION

I recently had the pleasure of viewing an inspiring documentary titled *Hasten Slowly: The Journey of Sir Laurens van der Post*. Sir Laurens spent a great deal of time with the Kalahari Bushmen, collecting their stories. For me, his extraordinary insights sum up in a few short paragraphs the essential wish that virtually all human beings harbor:

The Bushman in the Kalahari Desert talk about two "hungers."
There is the Great Hunger and there is the Little Hunger.
The Little Hunger wants food for the belly; but the Great Hunger,
the greatest hunger of all, is the hunger for meaning. . . .

There's ultimately only one thing that makes human beings deeply and profoundly bitter, and that is to have thrust upon them

a life without meaning. . . .
There is nothing wrong in searching for
happiness. . . .
But of far more comfort to the soul . . .
is something greater than happiness
or unhappiness, and that is meaning.
Because meaning transfigures all. . . .
Once what you are doing has for you
meaning,
it is irrelevant whether you're happy
or unhappy. You are content—you are not alone
in your Spirit—you belong.[1]

(Sir Laurens van der Post
from *Hasten Slowly,*
a film by Mickey Lemle)

As is related so eloquently, "the Great Hunger, the greatest hunger of all, is the hunger for meaning." *The Shift* is an invitation—both in this book and in the film of the same name—to explore the process of moving away from an aimless life to one filled with meaning and purpose.

I've been engaged for many years in helping people (including myself) reach their highest potential. I have now made almost 70 trips around our sun, and the one thing that stands out very clearly is that all of us want our lives to have purpose and meaning. In this book, I elucidate what seems to be required to reach a state of conscious, enlightened awareness that nurtures a life of purpose and meaning.

■ ■ ■

When the movie that this book is derived from was first released, it was titled *Ambition to Meaning*, yet many people were unclear about what those words meant or what the film was about. It seems that the title was a bit misleading, perhaps indicating that I'd made a documentary or just captured one of my lectures on film.

During the inaugural national tour when the movie was introduced to select audiences, I expressed my view about the title's confusion to the director and the executive producer. I said, "I love this movie; however, if I were doing it over, I'd give it a different title. I'd call it *The Shift*, because this term is referred to throughout the picture and is what has to take place for a person to move From Ambition To Meaning." To my delight—and to the credit of the director and producer—within a week the film had a new title. Even so, this notion of *From Ambition To Meaning* wouldn't go away.

As I contemplated how to present this essential message in a companion book to the movie, a deep meditation led me to use these four words as the book's organizational format. This is precisely what you now hold in your hands (or have on your book reader).

All of us on this glorious human voyage into adulthood have to make some shifts, or transitions, during the trip. Hopefully, we will go beyond the first two mandatory ones and move on to those shifts in consciousness that lead to a life filled with purpose. Now what do I mean by this?

The first shift that we all make takes us from nonbeing to being; from Spirit to form; from the invisible to our corporeal world of things, boundaries, and stuff. So, the first chapter of this book is titled "From. . . ." In my own humble (and, I'm certain, imperfect) fashion, I attempt to define the undefinable using words and phrases that are mere symbols of that which defies description. Nevertheless, it's what I've come to view as what that world of invisible Spirit, from which all things originate and to which they all return, looks like.

The next shift I portray is the shift from *From* to *Ambition*—thus, "Ambition . . ." is the title of Chapter 2. Ambition is the phase where we take on an ego self that is the opposite of the *place* of Spirit from which we came. Ego in this context is our false self.

These are two major and mandatory shifts that we undertake in this voyage of our humanness. Many of us reach the end of our life journey having only made those two transitions. Ambition, sadly, is often the end of the life story. In my film and in this book, I propose that there are two additional shifts available to all of us. When we proceed with them, the "life without meaning" that Sir Laurens referred to isn't the end of the story. We can all choose to make the leap past the second shift of the ego-driven ambition.

The third chapter is titled "To . . . ," signi-
fying arriving at a place in our minds where
we realize that we have an option to make
a U-turn away from the false self and begin
heading back in the direction of our origination—or what I'm calling our "Fromness."
This new phase of our life journey is a return
to Spirit and an invitation to the invisible
Divine realm to replace ego's dominance. We
learn how to tame ego as we head *To* a life of
meaning and purpose, nurtured by our Source
of being.

The shift described in Chapter 4 is "Meaning." As we abandon that false self and begin
our return trip back to Source while we're still
alive, we live by a new set of guidelines. We discover that the laws of the material world do not
necessarily apply in the presence of the *Meaning* that is encouraged by our shift to Source.
Manifestation of miracles and newly discovered
synchronicity begin to populate the landscape
of life. Indeed, Meaning is what now defines all
of the moments of our existence.

In my experience, unfortunately, ego's
Ambition is the final purpose of so many

lives—yet there are signs we can notice that signal those two additional shifts that release us from our illusion of ego comforts. We can do an about-face and head back to the place of Spirit in a third shift. And then, in the fourth shift, we achieve a life of Meaning and purpose by rededicating our Ambition to the fulfillment of our authentic self. We can ful-fill our greatest calling when we consciously undertake the journey From Ambition To Meaning. We can transform our individual lives and, as an additional bonus, influence the destiny of our sacred planet as well.

Sending love your way,
Dr. Wayne W. Dyer
Maui, Hawaii

CHAPTER ONE
FROM ...

*"And your body is the harp of your soul,
and it is yours to bring forth sweet
music from it, or confused sounds."*

— Kahlil Gibran[1]

For as long as I can remember, I've had a contemplative nature. When I was a little boy, I ruminated about life with questions that seldom had concrete answers. My first attempt to understand death was when Mr. Scarf, one half of the couple who ran the foster home where my brother David and I were living, passed away. After Mrs. Scarf told David and me that her husband had died, she handed both of us a banana as a kind of distraction from her grief. I immediately asked, "When will he be back?" Her one-word answer mystified me. "Never," she replied, wiping tears from what I perceived to be her ancient face.

I immediately went to my place on the top of our bunk beds, peeled my banana, and attempted to grasp what *never* meant. I imagined beginnings and endings, things like day and night ending and then beginning, and I thought of Mr. Scarf going to work and then coming home. In a rudimentary way, I recognized cause and effect, thinking about blossoms on fruit trees becoming apples or cherries. But I felt stymied by how Mr. Scarf could never come back. That totally disrupted what I knew at that age to be the natural flow of things. I lay on my top bunk staring at the ceiling, struggling to comprehend how Mr. Scarf could be gone forever.

Every time I thought of his never, ever coming back, I'd get a sick feeling in my stomach. My thoughts would then shift to something more palatable, something I could grasp, such as, *When will we have supper?* or *Where is my wagon?* But my naturally inquisitive mind continued pondering the mysterious and inexplicable idea of *forever,* and back would come a scary fluttering sensation in my stomach, which I feel even now as I write these words. Since Mr. Scarf died, I've written 34 books and given thousands of lectures on the essence of living a spiritual life, and I still get queasy when I recall those vivid childhood moments of trying to capture the meaning of life without a body to encapsulate it.

As I've pursued my writing and speaking activities over these many years, I've continued to be intrigued by what I call "the big questions." I've studied spiritual and philosophical masters from the East and West, in ancient and modern times, who have explored—and in many cases, lived—the truths that we view as our spiritual heritage. I love to contemplate these questions that have perplexed huma kind for as long as there has been recorded history (and, in all likelihood, even before that). The mystery of life remains fascinating and exciting to me. I enjoy entertaining the unanswerable, but I also feel peaceful with this conundrum.

One of those big questions is: *Who am I?* Part of the answer is that I'm a body with measurable characteristics. Yes, I have a name, talents, and accomplishments—but who I am also includes an intangible presence that I know is part of me. That aspect of myself doesn't have perceptible boundaries or a visible form. One name for this nonphysical aspect is *mind,* with its endless array of invisible thoughts percolating within the physical body.

My personal answer to the *Who am I?* question is that I'm a piece of the all-creating Source known by many names, including God, Spirit, Source, the Tao, Divine mind, and so on. Even though I can't see it or touch it, I know I'm a part of it, because I must be like what I came from—and what I came from is formless nothingness that merged into form. Therefore, I am both that invisible Spirit that is the Source of all, and simultaneously the form that's destined to return to the invisible.

Some other big questions I've also wrestled with are: *What happens after the death of my form? What is my life purpose? What does forever look like? Who or what is God?* I don't pretend to have definitive answers to these concerns. If great minds such as Lao-tzu, Socrates, Buddha, Rousseau, Descartes, Einstein, Spinoza, St. Francis, Rumi, Patanjali, Goethe, Shaw, Whitman, or Tennyson (among countless others) couldn't come up with the definitive answer, then certainly I'm not going to be able to clear up all of these mysteries in one book or even one lifetime. I can only offer my own interpretation of what I've come to know through study, living, and my concentrated efforts to make conscious contact with my Source of being, and with what I think of as the Source of everything in this material universe.

By far, the one question that has intrigued and puzzled me for as long as I can remember—the one that transcends the *Who am I? What is my purpose? What happens after death? Who or What is God?* questions—is the title of this first chapter, *From.* Where did I come *from?* For me, this has always been the *truly* big question.

Where Did I Come From?

When I think of the events that occurred and
the people that existed prior to my arrival on
planet Earth in 1940, I'm intrigued by what
determined my showing up at the precise time
I did. Where was I before my conception in
1939? What was I doing during the 12th and
13th centuries while the Crusades were taking place? Where was I in 2500 B.C. when
the pyramids were being constructed? What
or where was I millions of years ago before
human beings began appearing on this planet,
while the dinosaurs were roaming the earth?
Contemplating questions of this nature led
me to study a fair amount of the science that
explained how things come into form. While
I'm by no means an expert in this area, this is
what I've learned.

It is my understanding that quantum
physics regards this fact as scientifically unas-
sailable: that at the tiniest subatomic level,
particles themselves don't originate from a
particle. This means that matter originates
from something that is formless. Scientists

call the formlessness that produces matter "energy." This nonmaterial energy produced the particle that became who I am today. I think of this as a *shift from energy to form,* and as you read this book, I invite you to consider the shifts you've made to be who and where you are right now.

I think of the tiny little speck of human protoplasm that was my very first particle of humanity as being part of some kind of a "future-pull" that shifted into a fetus, and then into a baby, a toddler, a little boy, an adolescent, a young man, a mature adult, a middle-ager, and a person who has been alive for almost 70 years. All of those shifts were inherent in that originating energy that materialized as a microscopic particle and became me.

It's beyond my ability to fathom how such a miraculous unfolding could take place in the formation of who I am as a physical being. But I do believe that it transpired independently of my ability to do much about it other than simply observe my development. I am really and truly doing absolutely nothing. It seems truer to simply observe myself being lived by this all-creating energy that seems to do nothing, and at the same time leaves nothing undone. So where did that tiny little microscopic dot that was my first experience as a particle come from?

Remember that quantum physics tells us emphatically that particles do not come from particles. If we reduce that original particle to its subatomic status, it is smaller than chromosomes, atoms, electrons within the atom—and even the sub-sub-subatomic particles called quarks. Scientists have placed a quark the size of my origination point into a particle accelerator revved up to 250,000 mph and collided it with another quark. The result? Nothing was there. It appears that nothing exists at the moment of the transition to something. Or, as I enjoy saying, "From *nowhere* to *now here.*" All that exists in the world of *from* is pure formless energy—no particles.

Modern physics confirms the metaphysics of Genesis, which tells us that everything came from God and it was all good. Similarly, the Tao Te Ching tells us that all being originates in nonbeing. Thus, the question of where we came from is answered similarly by physics and metaphysics. They both conclude that we originated from something that has no form, no boundaries, no beginning, and no substance. We are all essentially spiritual beings having a temporary human experience. This is our essence. This is where we come from.

We Are What We Came From

In the movie version of *The Shift,* I have a brief discussion with several of the characters about this key concept: *Everything in the material world must be like what it came from, including each and every one of us.* In the film I refer to a slice of apple pie on a plate, asking, "What is that one piece of pie like?" The obvious answer is that it's like apple pie because it must be like what it came from. This is a familiar concept if we think of blood being drawn for a diagnostic test. A small syringe of blood provides medical practitioners with information about the entire supply of the person it was drawn from. Why? Because the sample must be like what it came from.

I extend this logic to myself and you as well. Since I didn't come from my parents, it isn't a logical conclusion to state that I must be like they are. Since I didn't come from my culture, my religion, or anything in this world, it isn't necessarily so that I must be the same as my surroundings or my society. But since I did come from an invisible energy Source that some call God, or Tao, or Divine mind, then I must be like what I came from. My conclusion about my origination is that I came from Spirit, and my true essence is that I am what I came from. I am a Divine piece of God. I am first and always a spiritual being inextricably connected to my Source of being.

Robert Burns summed this up poetically in his poem "New Year's Day," written in 1791:

The voice of Nature loudly cries,
And many a message from the skies,
That something in us never dies.[2]

That which is formless cannot be destroyed. The formless aspect of all beings exists in eternity, impervious to beginnings or endings. The truth seems to be that our essence is eternal, and it is only the physical body that appears to come and go in a cycle of birth and death. What we call birth and death are actually as inseparable as two sides of a coin, or daytime and nighttime. The question *Where did I come from?* is really only addressed to the *I* that is the physical body. But that physical aspect originated in nonbeingness.

We are exactly like the great Tao or God, and we have the freedom to make choices. Some of our choices cause our link to Source to become contaminated and rusty. One of those lackluster choices is believing that the expression of God through our physical self is an endpoint, or the ultimate, rather than an opportunity to choose how to express this gift. In this manner, we edge God out, and create an ego-driven life. The great lesson in this philosophical journey is to recognize our primary identity as a spiritual being who is eternal and therefore impervious to both birth and death.

Our physical self is an expression in the form of the energy of our spiritual essence; our real self is the loving observer of our sensory experiences. In order to fully harmonize with that essential nature, we must be dedicated to expressing its energy and be fully aware of the sacred choice we're making. For some, that will mean becoming more like God while temporarily housed in their body; for others, it will be creating godlike expressions of beauty, purpose, and wisdom in form.

The human voyage in bodily form is barely a parenthesis in the eternity of our real self. When the parenthesis closes, we're fully reimmersed in Spirit sans the materialized self. We're on that round-trip that Lao-tzu refers to in his famous line from the 40th verse of the Tao Te Ching: "Returning is the motion of the Tao." In the film version of *The Shift,* I quote from the T. S. Eliot poem "Little Gidding":

We shall not cease from exploration
And the end of all our exploring
Will be to arrive where we started
And know the place for the first time.[3]

But before we shed our physical body and complete this return trip, we can begin to understand our original nature by making an effort to be more like what we imagine our Source of being to be.

One way to conceptualize this is to imagine looking through a viewfinder that provides a clear picture of creative Source. Through these lenses, we see how it thinks, feels, and behaves. This view of our Source gives us a clearer view of our own true self.

Understanding the answer to *Where did I come from?* involves, more than anything else, attempting to live from a perspective that's in rapport with our original nature. We must become more like the spiritual nature of our origin. By recognizing the expression of Divine consciousness that is our physical being, we in turn make the choice of how to express that Divine spirit.

How Spirit Appears to Be

So often our physical world doesn't seem to be very spiritual, in spite of our having orig-

inated from spiritual essence. Henry Wads-
worth Longfellow expressed this dilemma in
his poem "A Psalm of Life":

> *Life is real! Life is earnest!*
> *And the grave is not its goal;*
> *Dust thou art, to dust returnest,*
> *Was not spoken of the soul.*[4]

The poet speaks of your life and mine as something beyond the physical, which he describes
as dust. We are all something other than what
we identify with our senses. There's no such
thing as a grave for our essential essence—our
spirit—but we may disregard and thus lose
touch with it. In fact, that's a pretty common
situation for all of us during different periods
of our lives when we choose to put our physical self in charge.

I love how another of my favorite poets,
Rabindranath Tagore, was able to describe in
two short lines what he thought was our most
important spiritual lesson:

> *God loves to see in me, not his servant,*
> *but himself who serves all.*[5]

The important questions we should be asking ourselves are: *Am I like God now? Am I getting closer? Am I there yet?*

If our true essence is Spirit, and we believe that is where we come from, it seems to me a simple task to reconnect to this authentic part of ourselves. One way to do this is to shift our thoughts and actions to the ways in which we imagine creative energy thinks and acts when its energy materializes in form. We need to be more like Spirit appears to be. Since this is what we came from, our Divinity is our destiny, regardless of how we've neglected it over the years. God or the great Tao, which we are all a part of, simply waits patiently for us to be like it is. I imagine that the all-creating Spirit, if indeed it had any wants for us, would want us to realize that.

An inspiring example of this is found in *The Quiet Mind: Sayings of White Eagle:*

> Your personal contribution towards the great plan for the evolution of man is to dwell continually upon the love of God; to look always into the light and so train yourself to recognize God's

goodness working through everyone else.

I don't believe that God is concerned with whether or not we show our love by building magnificent edifices for worship, by attending services, or through practicing rules laid down by religious organizations. It seems to me that if God were to speak to us, the message would simply be to love each other and offer reverence rather than enmity toward all of life.

■ ■ ■

The journey we've undertaken that has led us to this moment in this body encompasses something I'm calling "From." We come from something, somewhere, somehow; and it's a mystery to our little human minds, which tend to think in cause-and-effect ways. My conclusion is that if we're here now, there must have been a before, and certainly there will be an after.

I do, however, acknowledge the possibility that there's no before, no after, and no timeline. Everything may indeed be complete and all happening at once with no time, no space, no befores, and no afters. But I can't write from that perspective because *my* little human mind wants to make it all somewhat logical and comprehensible. Therefore, I'll describe "how Spirit appears to be" two distinct journeys. The first is the journey *from formless pure Spirit into form,* and the second is the journey *from a subatomic particle to birth.*

1. From Formless Pure Spirit into Form (Nonbeing to Being)

To write about nonbeing as the place we originate *from* requires me to imaginatively speculate on what the spiritual world of nonbeing is. The way I do this is to imagine a Divine consciousness who's in the business of manifesting form out of nothingness. Imagining a creation without a creator is a lot like trying to imagine a watch without a watchmaker. Observing creation every day, I cannot help but contemplate that it is from seeds that blossoms come, from blossoms come fruit, and from small acorns come giant oak trees. Despite my awe and lack of pure understanding, my curiosity about the world of pure Spirit continually plays with surmising the before and after—or "where from" and "where to" questions.

Nonbeing is a deliriously paradoxical state to contemplate, because I know in my heart that it surely exists, yet I only have my beingness with which to do the contemplating. I've already described my self-limitations concerning understanding the *From* of my existence. With that in mind, I offer you what I perceive "Fromness" to look like.

I conclude that everything is energy; it's all vibration at a variety of frequencies. The faster the vibration, the closer one is to Spirit and understanding where we came from. The pen I hold in my hand as I write these words appears to be solid, yet a glance at it through a powerful microscope shows that it's actually a field of moving particles, with mostly empty space between those particles. The vibrational makeup of my pen is energy that is slow enough to appear solid to my eyes, which can only perceive objects that fit within a certain frequency.

I hear the sounds of mynah birds as I write, and I know from my limited exposure to the laws of physics that sounds are a faster energy than my solid pen is. The light I see streaming in my window is an even faster energy, with tiny particles moving so fast as to appear to be green or blue or yellow, depending on how the rods and cones in my eyes are calibrated to pick up these energetic signals. Beyond the frequencies of light are the vibrational energies of thought.

Yes, thought is an energy system. The highest-calibrated frequencies of thought, which are measured through simple kinesiology methods, reveal that faster vibrations approach the ultimate in energy vibration—the dimension of Spirit itself. The highest vibrational thoughts are aligned with the Source energy of the Tao or God. When experienced as thoughts, these faster vibrations create strength, but slower thoughts create a weaker response in kinesiology tests.

The way this works is when we focus mental energy on a thought aligned with Source and raise an arm to shoulder height as a test of our strength, it's difficult for any-one to lower it. When we focus our men-tal energy on slower-frequency thoughts, however, our upraised arm is easily pushed down by another person. When it comes to kinesiology, every negative emotion makes the physical body weaker. These studies are graphic examples of the world of nonbeing, and they're also opportunities to explore the frequencies that harmonize with the vibra-tions of Source energy.

That field from which all things originate and to which all things return has a *feel* to it. Based on the research and ruminations of some of the most revered beings who have walked this earth, creation itself isn't an act of violence—it's a pleasurable, joyful act. There doesn't appear to be any fear, shame, blame, anger, humiliation, anxiety, or hatred associ-ated with the workings of the great Tao that seems to be doing nothing and yet leaving nothing undone.

Remember that the body we live in 24/7 wasn't created by a human being; it's a creation of God. So it makes perfect sense to me that if our body, God's creation, is filled with negative thoughts, it would be weak. Simply expressing a falsehood weakens a strong person's arm; expressing the truth always creates a strong physical response because truth is of God. How could creation or the Creator create from an untruthful perspective? There's abundant literature based on rigorous research in kinesiology that nonbeing, the place that we came from, is aligned with energy that is strongest when expressing truth.

The highest/fastest vibrating thought that will always keep us strong is the energy of love. My conclusion is that nonbeing and love are synonymous. Mysticism and virtually all religions state that the Supreme Being is love and the only pure truth is love. Some religions trivialize the Supreme Being by inventing a god in the image and likeness of humans. Theirs is a deity of endless nit-picking rules Who is easily offended; always being sinned against; and prone to anger, revenge, and punishment. The love I'm speaking of personifies nonbeing, accessed and incorporated within us from where we originated. It has no rules, doesn't wish to control, never punishes, and doesn't know how to descend into anti-love expressions.

The entire universe, as I see it, is made of love; and each of us appears to be an individualized expression of the One Being of Love. Simplified: *God is love.* I like Ralph Waldo Emerson's description of love as a synonym for God. What an incredibly magnificent concept—this idea of nonbeing existing as a state of pure, indescribable bliss, and one that is necessary for the act of creation to take place.

Think about it: we came from love; therefore, we must be love in some way, since we must be like what we came from. Jesus put it this way: "He who does not love does not know God, for God is love" (1 John 4:8). Pretty basic, and very straightforward. Nonbeing is love. Since we came from nonbeing, we must be love.

But we somehow manage to move away from our original nature. Every thought of nonlove is a movement away from where we came from. Every act of judgment, anger, shame, fear, anxiety, and violence is a movement toward not loving and not knowing, God. Even an anti-love thought is a movement away from our original nature.

What was it like to be in that state of pure love awaiting our transition into being-ness? What were we doing? Once we acquire form, these questions are almost impossible to contemplate. However, here is my concep-tualization of what nonbeingness feels like before we journey into this world of form and boundaries:

— **Nothingness.** The one thing we can certainly agree on is that we had nothing. There was nothing to own, nothing to do, nothing to fight, nothing to worry about; we were nothing in physical terms. This idea of nothing is really difficult for us. We've entered a world where something has replaced noth-ing; where form replaced nonform. In our material world, owning nothing and doing nothing are generally interpreted as signs of

failure. Yet our true essence is most comfortable with nothing.

It seems to me that the most efficient way
to know and experience where we came from
is to make every effort to reconnect to nothing by creating the experience of no attachments, no things, and no thoughts. We do
this by simply being, rather than doing and
accumulating. As Herman Melville is believed
to have said, "God's one and only voice is
silence," and this is an invitation to experience
our original world of nothing. All of creation
emerges from the silent void, as does every
sound. Every bit of light comes from nothingness; every thought emerges from nonthought.
There's a Zen proverb that reminds us that
it's the silence between the notes that makes
the music. Without silence to interrupt the
sounds, there can be no music—it would be
only one long, continuous tone. But of course
even the long tone originated in the void.

Nothingness is equivalent to the expression
of zero, mathematically: It can't be divided; it
has no empirical value; and if we multiply
anything by it, we get a sum of nothing. Yet

without the indivisible zero, mathematics itself would be impossible. Before we came into this material world, our essence was nothing. We had no things encumbering us—no rules, no duties, no money, no parents, no hunger, no fear . . . nothing at all.

When I wrote essays on the 81 verses of the Tao Te Ching for my book *Change Your Thoughts—Change Your Life,* I was struck by how much emphasis Lao-tzu placed on knowing the great Tao (God) by giving up everything, letting go of all attachments, doing less, owning nothing, and practicing getting to know God by emptying rather than filling the mind. Almost every great spiritual master tells us to find God in emptiness, and to hear God speak to us in silence. So one of the answers to the question of where we come from is: nowhere, with nothing.

We must make the effort to find our way to that peaceful nothingness while we're still in our body. We can empty our pockets or purse, but we especially need to empty our *mind* and relish the joy of living in our physical world while simultaneously experiencing the bliss

of nothingness. This is our origin, just as it
is assuredly our ultimate destination as well.
Albert Einstein once noted that everything is
emptiness, and form is condensed emptiness.
And according to my teacher Nisargadatta
Maharaj:

> This is real liberation: to know that
> you are nothing. All your knowledge,
> including yourself, is liquidated—then
> you are liberated.[6]

— **Oneness.** Closely aligned with nothingness is the idea of oneness. How can it be that
at our spiritual core, we're both nothing, as
well as connected to something called oneness? Everything in this physical universe of
ours is in some way connected to everything
else, because it all originated from the void of
nothingness. There aren't several of these voids
to choose from—we came from the same void
that everyone and everything else came from.
When we attempt to isolate anything, we find
that it is in some way part of everything else
in the universe. Just as it is absurd for a single

wave to see itself as separate from the ocean, so it is for any of us not to recognize our oneness with what we know as infinity.

Oneness is difficult to adequately comprehend because we're so immersed in a world of things that seem *other* to us. The opening line of the Tao Te Ching suggests that the Tao that can be named is not the eternal Tao. In other words, as soon as it's named, it's lost, because we've created a dichotomy. Oneness means just that: only one. As I said earlier, just like zero in mathematics, it can't be divided or subdivided. The instant we label or name it, it's something else, separate; consequently, it's not the unity of oneness. Lao-tzu repeatedly mentions that when we name it, we've lost it. In oneness, there are no names; there's only the one. That's why it's so impossible to write about oneness—every word I use to describe it illustrates that I'm not comprehending it!

The place that we came from is devoid of dichotomies, unlike our material world, which is dependent on pairs of opposites. In this world, without a concept of up, there can be no down. Without an idea of death, there's no life. The north pole of a magnet can't exist without the south pole. No male, no female. No right, no wrong. We think in dichotomies, and we identify ourselves on the basis of opposites. We know what we like, what tastes good, what feels good, and so on, because of our experience with what we dislike. Because of this material world, many of us find it difficult to access oneness, the world that the ancient teacher Hermes described in this way:

> God is one. And he that is one is nameless; for he does not need a name, since he is alone. . . . All things have been derived from One . . .[7]

The idea of oneness is next to impossible to grasp because we live in a world of contrasts, and contrast requires more than one element. So here we are, persistently in our world of twoness. How can we grasp the idea of oneness in the world of nonbeing that we occupied before we came into beingness? One way might be to think of our fingers, legs, arms, toes, and

eyes: We don't think of them as separate entities from our total being. We don't refer to our
fingers as being separate from ourselves. Even
though they have their unique qualities and
character, they're part of the oneness we refer
to as ourselves. So it is with our relationship
to Source or God before we came into this
world—in that world, which I'm calling our
"Fromness," we and God were one.

Oneness as the concept of where we're
from means discarding all ideas of separation
from anything and anyone. We can simulate
oneness through the part of ourselves that
knows the silence where there are no names
and no things. Here, we can begin to feel our
connection to everyone, to the earth, to the
universe, and ultimately to the great Tao. Oneness becomes accessible in that great power,
which acts without doing, keeps the entire
universe in order, and generates form from
nothingness.

If we imagine that we're free of all labels,
all separation, and all judgments about this
world and the life inhabiting it, we can begin
to understand oneness. The place we want to

enter is of simply *being*. We can picture the
Source of being as an energy that's as available
to us as is the sky. There's no anger toward anyone or anything because everyone and everything is Spirit. This Spirit is God, our Source of
being. We are it, and it is who we are. We relax
into the silence of where we came from. We
discover the meaning of life by being able to
return to the oneness and nothingness while
still in material form, without having to leave
our body in the ritual of death. The closer we
get to experiencing our original nature, the
more peace and purpose flows through us.

2. From a Subatomic Particle to Birth (Earliest Beingness to Birth)

We've examined the logic and spiritual specu-
lation of what our nonbeingness might look
like. Please remember that this is largely my
interpretation of the invisible world of Spirit,
which is both our originating source and our
place of return when our physical self is no
longer animated by Divine consciousness.

In one magically mysterious nanosecond, we made the transition from nonbeing to being. A subatomic particle of human proto-plasm emerged from Spirit, and everything that was needed for the journey we call life was taken care of. An invisible force that I call a future-pull was set in motion, filling in our physical characteristics. Our ultimate height; body shape; eye, skin, and hair color; wrinkles that would someday appear; and, of course, the business of our body ceasing to be alive, were all arranged, without our having to do a thing about it.

In the film *The Shift,* I speculate that if everything needed for the physical journey is handled by the nameless nothingness, then it isn't beyond my capacity to hypoth-esize that everything needed to fulfill our entire destiny also arose in that moment of transition from nonbeing to beingness. Our dharma—our essential purpose for being here—our personality, and all of the help we'd need along the way were also in that microscopic dot. If our body was on a jour-ney that's all handled by the great Tao or

God, then I say, why not everything else
about us as well?

The primary characteristic of this nine-
month journey is what I call *surrender*. There
was nothing for us to do. Somehow, our Source
of being in its infinite wisdom was going to do
it all. We and our birth mother allowed the
great Tao to do what it does. The truth is that
we were doing nothing; we were simply being
done. In that entire nine-month voyage, we
were *lived* by the Tao. Understanding where
we came from and where we'll return to is
really experiencing the feeling of total surrender. This means allowing the force that's
doing everything to simply do it without
interference.

In that first nine months of our life as a
microscopic dot, and then as a growing embryo,
we and our mother practiced noninterference.
Our natural wisdom knew that all we needed
in order to thrive and flourish was being taken
care of by the unseen force that appeared to
do nothing and yet left nothing undone. We
didn't have to be concerned about when our
fingernails would show up, and if they'd grow

at the ends of our fingers rather than behind our ears. Our heartbeat began right on time, without our needing to make arrangements to turn it on. By surrendering and allowing, we were being formed into the perfection that we signed up for while we were ensconced in non-being. The energy responsible for our beingness knew precisely what to do and when to do it. This is our authentic self.

From the moment of conception, we were swaddled in the arms of invisible infinite wisdom. We allowed our true self to unfold in the perfect design that was inherent in both our nonbeing and our beingness. Had we stayed completely immersed in that state of consciousness, we would have remained aligned with our Source. In that scenario, there's no occasion to wonder about our life purpose. That little speck that we were didn't know anything about accumulating, achieving, or having ambition. It simply was *being,* allowing itself to surrender to the invisible force that administers everything.

But rather than staying in that state of allowing and surrender, we were hooked by a set of beliefs that put ambition ahead of allowing. The part of us that is from allowing, surrendering, and being . . . arrived in form in a place where ambition was given primary importance. Had we been capable of continuing our life with what we came from, we'd be living at the highest levels of awareness or God-realization. Enlightenment would be ours, and it seems to have been intended that way. As Jesus put it, "Even the least among you can do all that I have done and even greater things," and, "Is it not written in your law, 'I said, you are gods'?" (John 10:34). Indeed, where we came from is God and, therefore, we're God as well.

The reality seems to be that we all tend to shift to ambition in a form that we insist on directing. The possibility is that we all have the choice to then shift to meaning and thereby complete our return to the place I call "From." In the next chapter, I'll discuss the Ambition phase.

■   ■   ■

Here's a recap of, and suggestions for, recapturing our "Fromness":

— **Nothingness.** Allow yourself to enjoy silence and meditation. Even if you don't have a structured meditation practice, give yourself time to simply savor the silence. Turn off the noisemakers at home and in your auto. Create time to be in nature away from human-made sounds. Learn to treat your voyages inward as sacred space, spending moments repeatedly letting go by physically and mentally relaxing. Let go of worrying, planning, thinking, recalling, wondering, hoping, desiring, or remembering. Consciously let go of each physical sensation you notice. Do this one moment at a time. Enter a state where you can let your possessions, your family, your home, your work, and your body cease to exist. Experience the inner bliss of nothingness.

When you emerge from your silence, begin the process of detachment by literally giving away something that you don't use at least once every day. In nothingness, you will find greater intimacy with your Source of being.

— **Oneness.** Begin to view yourself as connected to every person you encounter by valuing and loving the part of you that flows through all life. Feel your connection to all of nature and practice nonjudgment and love, beginning with yourself. This means that when you feel offended or upset, instead of directing your attention toward the person or incident outside of you, notice what it is that *you* are feeling, and where you feel it in your body. Redirect your attention from external circumstances to an examination of just how that particular upset feels in your body. This is how you begin practicing oneness. Set your inner barometer on love and acceptance for the feelings you're experiencing. Remind yourself that you are one with God and, therefore, *you* are love. That is all you have to offer; so begin with loving the hurt, offended, or upset parts of yourself.

As you integrate all of yourself, assembling the parts into the oneness that is you, you'll discover the impossibility of your being separate from anyone else on our planet. Simply recognizing the times of anger or annoyance as opportunities to know yourself better, and to forgive and love yourself, will extend your awareness of the oneness you are. Practice this kind of oneness, and love will flow outward naturally to include others whom you've previously judged.

— **Surrender.** Practice the art of allowing. Watch your body as it goes through its motions. The hair changing to gray or falling out, the skin sagging . . . the little changes that happen on their own, independent of your opinion about them. Then practice the same kind of noninterference with your family, your friends, your co-workers—everyone. The Beatles had it right—there will be an answer if you just let it be. This is surrender. This is the art of giving up your need to control your world and everyone in it.

As we in the recovery movement have been saying for many years, "Let go and let God." When you practice surrender on a daily basis, everything seems to fall into place. You came from a place of well-being—of love, kindness, gentleness, joy, and purity. This is your "Fromness." Surrender to it. When I find myself wanting to control my destiny, I say to myself, "Let go, Wayne. Let go and let God!" Try this using your own name—it works!

My attempts to describe where we come from are stated in the 21st verse of the Tao Te Ching:

The greatest virtue is to follow the Tao and the Tao alone.

The Tao is elusive and intangible.
Although formless and intangible,
it gives rise to form.
Although vague and elusive,
it gives rise to shapes.
Although dark and obscure,
it is the spirit, the essence,
the life breath of all things.

Throughout the ages, its name has been preserved
in order to recall the beginning of all things.
How do I know the ways of all things at the beginning?
I see what is within me.

■ ■ ■

I close this chapter on your "Fromness" by citing my very favorite passage from *A Course in Miracles* (pages 486 to 488). It reminds us all that knowing where we came from is a function of *remembering,* and that we cannot unlock the mysteries of our spiritual origins unless we move to a place where we can, in fact, *remember* our Source of being, right here, right now:

The *memory* of God comes to the quiet mind.
It cannot come where there is conflict; for a mind at war against itself *remembers* not eternal gentleness. . . .
What you *remember* is a part of you.
For you must be
as God created you. . . . Let all this madness be undone
for you, and turn in peace of the *remembrance* of God, still shining in your quiet mind.

Study this passage carefully and you will unlock the mystery that is your true Source of being. Get quiet, let go of conflict, become

peaceful, and remember the eternal gentleness
that resides within you.

■   ■   ■   ■   ■

CHAPTER TWO
AMBITION...

*"All unhappiness is due to the ego.
With it comes all your trouble. If you would
deny the ego and scorch it by ignoring
it you would be free. . . ."*

— Ramana Maharshi[1]

Before the moment of birth, and before our Ambition phase kicks in, each of us is completely aligned with God or the Tao—or whatever name we choose to call the Source of our being. In that pre-form stage of "Fromness," Ambition isn't something we entertain—we have no goals, no aspirations. There's nothing we have to do or take care of, no one to impress or defeat . . . all we need to do is just *be*. Our existence in the experience of "From" is precisely what our Source of being intended: free of interference. We are our authentic self. At that stage, we are as much like God as most of us have ever been since.

In the movie version of *The Shift,* I describe how we move away from our authentic self (our Divinity), and adopt a false one. We come in to this world a perfect creation, but for many reasons, we're encouraged to leave this authentic self behind and to take on a false one. We, and those responsible for our parenting, often disregard that our destiny and all we need to fulfill our dharma is built in to us. With good intentions, we're seduced into becoming a self that is diametrically opposed to who we are authentically.

The Nature of Our False Self

Imagine a creature proceeding through its developmental journey in form here on Earth, learning and believing that it is something other than what it came here to be. Take, for example, a baby hyena who's told by parental figures that he really isn't a hyena. This baby hyena is forbidden to follow his natural inclinations to frolic, sharpen his teeth, stalk prey, run with the pack, hunt in a group, make noise, or chew the carcasses of animals he's killed. Instead, the young hyena's parents have told him to stop all of the weird behavior like laughing and howling and to sit still while the other hyenas hunt—in other words, to believe that he's something he's not.

The point is that everything that's part of creation has a dharma. No animal, bird, insect, fish, or plant can cultivate a false self or believe that it's something other than what the creative Source intended. There's still no evidence to doubt what Emerson once noted in his journal: "All the thoughts of a turtle are turtle." Emerson was making the same point that I am here: that all of God's creatures are authentic and can only be what their dharma intended them to be. Are human beings an exception to God's intention? Some aspects of our development pose that question.

We didn't continue to unfold as creation determined, in the same way we did in those first nine months inside our mother's womb. Following that developmental time, we were greeted by parents, a culture, and a host of well-meaning folks representing religious, educational, and commercial interests. They held us, admired the miracle of creation, and looked heavenward, saying, *Great work, God! Absolutely, amazingly perfect. Thank You, thank You, thank You! But now we'll take over from here.* Thus began our shift to the bizarre twisted world of Ambition.

We received metaphorical training wheels and became trainees in the vigorous effort to convince ourselves that we're not a part of Divine consciousness. In the shift to become part of the world of Ambition, we learned to aspire to something totally alien to our "Fromness." This path required us to reidentify ourselves in ways that no hyena or turtle would ever imagine doing!

The shift to Ambition requires humans to cultivate an ego, to edge God out. We're trained to believe that who we truly are is whatever our ego convinces us is our true self. We spend more than half of our life, on average, believing in and relying on the training we underwent concerning the importance of having Ambition. The next big shift is when we realize that a false self only offers empty promises and a guarantee of self-recrimination and futility (which will be discussed in the next two chapters).

For now, let's look at what that false self teaches us as we traverse the path of ego and learn to believe in the importance of Ambition as a way of defining who we are.

Taking on an Ego

As we emerge from the world of Spirit at the moment of birth, we begin the perilous journey of acquiring an identity that's virtually the opposite of our true self. I call this development of the ego or the false self the "Ambition period." It's a sharp contrast to our "Fromness," where Ambition was unknown largely because we simply allowed ourselves to be lived by the great Tao.

Thus begins the journey from being nobody—and feeling content with our nobody status—to being immersed in a curriculum that my friend Ram Dass calls "somebody training." Ego insists that we traverse from nothing to something, from being no one to being someone, from oneness to twoness, from unity to separation. It is this journey that requires us to edge God out and learn to believe in a false self. Ego's number one job at this stage is eliminating our nobody status by encouraging Ambition and creating a new (albeit false) identity.

The quotation that opens this chapter introduces us to the ego as the cause of our troubles. If we want to know pure happiness and live a blissful life, we need to do as Sri Ramana Maharshi says and learn to *scorch* ego by ignoring it. But ego is adept at resisting our efforts to ignore it, and it will do everything it can to prevent us from sacrificing our somebody status. Ego wants us to be a somebody who is more important than the other somebodies!

I've isolated six components of the ego, the false self. They're what our ego tells us to convince us that we're something other than the nobody we might have remained. Beginning with infancy and throughout our somebody training, we learn to believe in them.

Here is a thorough explanation of each of the six lies that the ego wants us to believe:

1. "Who I Am Is What I Have"

Early on, we get the message that having nothing is the equivalent of being a human being without any value as a person. As we grow into this component of ego identification, we learn that the more stuff we accumulate, the more important we are. Our self-concept shifts from feeling that we're valuable because we exist as a piece of God to assessing our worthiness on the basis of how many toys we own, their monetary worth, and how prestigious they're assumed to be by other somebodies in our culture.

In the movie of *The Shift,* a well-to-do couple—who own many lavish toys and flaunt their cars, clothes, homes, and country-club memberships—evaluates their success in life on the basis of their extensive inventory of possessions. Yet it is clear that they have an equally disproportionate sense of their own selves. The more stuff they accumulate, the more they have to worry about, which results in chasing after more stuff, and on and on the merry-go-round goes. This finally culminates in a very poignant moment in the film in which the husband begins to wonder if his whole life has been wrong.

It's a compelling question to consider. What if we spent our entire life chasing after the symbols of success, collecting more, and always striving to get something bigger and better than our neighbors? The mantra of the ego is *more*. It seems to scream out at us from deep within, "You'll be happy once you win something else, something more expensive, something that will give you prestige and power!" This accumulation mentality begins with our childhood toys. If we don't recall our own childhood, we can see and hear a portrayal of how it is expressed by today's toddlers: "These are *my* toys! That's *mine!*"

When we become adults, our larger and more expensive versions of toys epitomize our success. When these possessions are lost or threatened, we feel that our value as human beings is diminished. The same holds true when someone else has more than we do, or when we can't afford to acquire more stuff. The problem that exists with this mind-set of evaluating ourselves on the basis of what we've acquired is this: *If we are what we have, then when we don't have, we aren't!*

The ego is a tough taskmaster. As far as it is concerned, our very worth is at stake. Of course we know that we came here with nothing, and we'll take nothing with us when we go. Yet during our life, ego manages to imprison us. If we let it, our stuff rules us and determines our value. It's not uncommon for people whose identity depends on ego values to fall into depression and even commit suicide when their stuff is threatened or disappears. One of my favorite lines in the Tao Te Ching reminds us that what we gain causes more trouble than what we lose, and that by being content, we'll never be disappointed.

This kind of thinking doesn't sit well with the ego, because it's the part of us that believes our very essence is tied in with what we have, and there can be no contentment when our stuff is taken away. This is why so many people who strive for more and more feel discontent and anguished, and ultimately view themselves as failures when their inventory of stuff is diminished in any way.

Where we come from and where we return to is a place where our stuff is unnecessary in order to feel joy and contentment. Whatever came our way as a fetus and an unspoiled child gave us a great sense of fulfillment.

I used to watch my young children express so much joy playing with a cardboard box or a spool of yarn or some napkins. They could get lost in just watching a fluttering butterfly or a tiny ant on the sidewalk. They were filled with wonder at virtually anything that came into their field of awareness. This is a remnant of our "Fromness"—we were that way, too. We should take to heart the advice of the Persian poet Rumi: "Sell your cleverness and purchase bewilderment."

Our obsessiveness about owning more and more and boasting of our possessions is an indication that we've allowed our false self to become the dominant force in our life. When the false self defines us, it means we're defined by something that isn't true. It's a spiritually bankrupt way to run our life. Who we are has nothing to do with things or even our physical self. We need nothing to verify or validate us. We're infinite individualized expressions of God—period. Things and so-called ownership do not verify who we are. *We are what we have* is ego's false belief, which is encouraged by our culture.

2. "Who I Am Is What I Do"

Early in life, we learn that what we do and how well we do it can be used to define us in a favorable way. *She actually grabbed my finger, and she's only six hours old! He made eye contact with me; he's so alert. She picked up her toy and held it at three months. He took his first step. She said her first words.* There are thousands of things like these that earned us praise and let us know how special and wonderful we were. This is all the work of the ego striving to direct us. We learn that doing things—especially if we do them earlier and better than others—is rewarding. We learn to be more of a human *doing* than a human *being* (who just has to *be*). A human doing is evaluated on the basis of what he or she does and how it stacks up with all of the other doers. I'm not intending this observation to be critical or judgmental. I only want to point out that having ambition to be a doer was a top priority in our developmental years.

With each task that we mastered (such as crawling, walking, talking, becoming potty trained, riding a tricycle and then a bicycle, and learning to tie our shoes), we took on an identity that told us, "When you do things—and do them better and sooner than your counterparts—then you have value." We were rewarded for our accomplishments with praise, candy, money, or whatever our particular family used in order to reward us.

Again, I feel a need to point out that none of this reinforcement for performing is bad; it simply teaches the aspiring human to believe the ego's personalized message of "You are what you do," which is blatantly false. You are *not* what you do. If you never did a thing in your entire life, you'd still be a spiritual being having a human experience rather than the other way around.

Ego craves confirmation of our value through indicators; Spirit operates on a totally different basis. *Home* is beyond ego, as the spiritual entity known as Emmanuel says:

> *Your mind does not know the way*
> *Your heart has already been there.*
> *And your soul has never left it.*
> *Welcome home.*[2]

Our early teaching convinces us that who we are is defined by our accomplishments. Our educational system emphasizes accomplishment, reinforcing the idea even more. *No gold star* is easily interpreted as *no value as a person.* When we fail a test, our sense of self is a feeling of failure, and such ego-strengthening notions become our reality. From preschool through graduate school, the messages are similar: We're defined by how well we do. If we don't do well, we're labeled "underachievers." The concept of Ambition as an indicator of how much worth we have, both in the eyes of our fellow humans and even in the mind of God, is cemented firmly into our consciousness.

These ideas carry over into every aspect of our developing ego. The popular saying "Winning isn't everything, it's the only thing" makes losers out of 50 percent of competitors, since every competition that has a winner must also have a loser. In all areas of life, whatever we do tends to define our worth. The artist whose portfolio is judged inferior to another's often feels a loss of value as a human being. The singer who doesn't make it to number one in some category feels that he or she is worth less.

Ego training continues into adulthood, often eradicating any self-concept based on our Divinity as a piece of God who came from nondoing and is headed back to nondoing. Ego training contributes to a self-concept that makes us shrivel into a feeling of insignificance at our meager portfolio in contrast to those who have achieved more. The truth is that we don't have to do a thing in order to validate ourselves as worthy and valuable. Had we done nothing but just be godlike, we'd fulfill our own dharma. Ironically, we would most likely have created a larger and more impressive résumé.

At this very moment, I'm writing without doing. That's right. I simply allow ideas to come through me and onto this page. I'm not busy writing, trying, struggling, working, or any other *doing*—I'm simply letting go and letting God, just as I do with my heart, my lungs, my circulatory system, and everything else that the physical me comprises. I let myself be, not by thinking big and setting gigantic goals, but by recalling Lao-tzu's advice in the Tao Te Ching:

> *The practice of the Tao involves daily diminishing;*
> *decreasing until nothing is being done.*
> *When nothing is being done, ironically, nothing can be left undone.*

True mastery of the world can be attained
by allowing things to take their natural course.
It can never be attained by interfering.

Yes, this is indeed paradoxical, and it points exactly to the way that all of creation takes place. God is doing nothing, yet leaving nothing undone. If we dissuade ego by *scorching it with inattention,* we accomplish what we came here to do and be, by *being* rather than *doing.* Our fingernails grow, our food digests, and our heart beats without our doing something to make those things happen.

In the movie *The Shift,* David, the frustrated filmmaker, illustrates what I'm writing about. His character acts out problems that arise with his ego belief: *I am what I do.* If he can't make his movie, he loses not only his happiness, but his soul as well. It's only when David begins to let go, to take a few moments to be present *in* the present and let in the ideas that are being taught in the film, that the *magic* begins to take hold. I repeat what will become a familiar theme: *If we are what we do, then when we don't or can't, we aren't.* I think we need to pay special attention to this point.

Most people raised in the modern world are skeptical of doing nothing. We're weaned on Ambition, and particularly the "doing more" expression of it. Yet we need to consider the very real and troubling aspects of believing that we are what we do.

In the film, David loses his sense of self-worth because of ego's teachings. He becomes depressed and feels totally lost—all because he's bought in to ego's teachings that he's defined as a worthy individual on the basis of what he accomplishes. For David, then, not having the film project he wants causes him to feel that he's not a person of value. It's a false conclusion based on living from the false self.

This is the danger of listening to ego rather than our authentic self. Every time we feel as though we've failed, we place our worth as a human being in jeopardy. If we're sick or injured and can no longer perform according to our standards, we also become candidates for depression or are susceptible to a multitude of physical ailments. As we go through the process of watching our body age naturally, we'll notice a gradual lessening of our physical skills. It's highly likely that the members of the generation behind us will even surpass our achievements, which happens routinely in competitive sports such as swimming and running. Ultimately, no longer able to be the doer that we once were, it seems that our worthiness as a human "doing" has evaporated. That scenario is only true if we listen to a false master—our ego.

I've reached the age that many refer to as "retirement time." But I've practiced the scorching of my ego in this regard for several decades. I'm not my work. I'm not my accomplishments. I'm not my résumé. I live, breathe, and work from my authentic self. As I've said here, and in many of my previous writings, I do not *do* writing—I *am* writing, and writing is me. I simply follow Lao-tzu's advice to be lived by the great Tao that animates all things by doing nothing. This being the case, how is the concept of retirement even possible? How can I retire from who I am? And who I am allows

this writing and speaking and everything else
I do to take place.

My advice on relinquishing ego's assump-
tions that we are what we do is to live from our
most authentic self. Then when we're able, we
must replace Ambition with Meaning. When
we make the shift to Meaning, we see the
absurdity of ever being able to retire from
who we are. I've always appreciated Picasso's
observation on evaluating ourselves on the
basis of what we do: "While I work," he said,
"I leave my body outside the door, the way
Moslems take off their shoes before entering
the mosque."[3] We can treat our work like that,
by leaving our body outside and letting our
soul *do*.

3. "Who I Am Is What Others Think of Me"

Throughout life, we're bombarded by ego messages attempting to convince us that our worth
comes from the observations and opinions of
others. Once again, this false self proclaims

as truth that something or someone external to us is responsible for our validation. And again, it's necessary to remind ourselves who we truly are. We're Divine pieces of the whole, individualized expressions of God created out of the great void. Our authentic self is the same as that which it came from. Our connection to our Divine self remains healthy and strong as long as we recognize and repudiate the false idea that validation of our self-esteem is external to our being.

Unfortunately, it's true that we're taught from an early age to believe the opinions of others more than our own opinions of ourselves. Our parents, siblings, friends, and teachers—in some cases, everyone in our young lives—are held in higher esteem than we are. We're convinced that if anyone in those groups disapproves of us, we should respect his or her viewpoint over our own. This immersion in the false teachings of the ego gradually erodes our sense of worth, causing us to doubt our Divinity.

Self-esteem stems from internally held positive beliefs about ourselves, not from the approval of others. Ego's worldly survival guide dictates that we're physical beings without a core spirituality. It pursues the false idea that our value is determined by what others choose to think about us. If we truly know who we are, we can ignore those ego messages and simply regard the opinions of our fellow humans for what they are—simply their opinions.

Unfortunately, ego tries (more often than not, quite successfully) to ward off our awareness of our spiritual nature. Unaware of its influence, we spend a lot of time trying to win the approval of everyone we meet. When we don't receive that approval, we begin to internalize those external assessments and expend large chunks of our life trying to be what we think someone else wants us to be.

Believing that who we are is defined by what other people think of us cripples the joyful spontaneity of our authentic selves. If others disapprove, and their opinion defines us, then we modify ourselves or shrink from view. Our image of ourselves is located in them, and when they reject us, we no longer "are" at all. The ego's way of dealing with this dilemma is to adapt to everyone else's opinions. If they think we're stupid, we attempt to convince them to think otherwise by trying to be the person they want us to be. We cease to exist except as a reflection of what others think.

The fact is that who you are has absolutely nothing to do with any thoughts or opinions that exist in anyone else in this world. Period. That person whose approval you desperately sought could change his mind tomorrow; and instead of thinking that you're intelligent, talented, and beautiful . . . might decide you're a foolish dolt who's unappealing to be around. If you listen to your authentic self, you'll be completely unaffected by such judgments. However, if your false self dominates your thinking, you'll be miserably affected. This is how ego lures you into disregarding your authentic self.

When approval-seeking is the guiding principle of life, it's virtually impossible to achieve a loving relationship with another human being. We can't give away what we don't have. We can't give love and respect to others when we have to find it for ourselves in the judgments of others. Ego contributes to a constant state of fear, confusion, and unhappiness.

So, what does all of this approval-seeking and low self-esteem have to do with Ambition? The short answer is that we're taught to pursue the approval and validation of virtually everyone in positions of authority throughout our life with as much Ambition as possible. Ambition almost always means putting our own life and opinions in the background. We learn to please parents, teachers, professors, authority figures, and bosses. And how is this accomplished? By ranking their opinions above our own. This is a process that's performed day in, day out; month in, month out; and year in, year out, often on a subconscious level. The result is an ego-based, false self.

When we give more credence to the opinions of others than to our own self-assessments, we deny the very wisdom that created us. The more we integrate these egoistic beliefs, the more we tend to believe in our own self-importance. Our drive to accumulate and achieve ultimately causes us to forget that our intrinsic value is our connection to our spiritual self. In other words, our connection to our Source of being becomes obscured in favor of pleasing ego's ideas that we are what other people's egos think of us!

This has been a significant lesson for me to learn over the years. When I speak or write, I encounter opinions that vary from my own. I know that if I speak to a thousand people, there will be a thousand separate opinions of me in that audience. My reputation isn't located in me, it's in the people who read and listen to what I have to say. Consequently, I've learned not to be concerned about my reputation. Since it isn't located *in* me, I put my attention on my own character instead of how others view me. My primary relationship in life is to my Source of being (to God, if you will). "Do not imagine that anyone can have true faith in God who has not faith in himself," is a saying from Paramananda, which strongly resonates with me. If I choose to give up faith in myself by listening to the entreaties of my ego, then I cannot have faith in my Source of being—they're always intertwined.

These first three components of ego *(who I am is what I have, what I do, and what others think of me)* focus on its desire to build up our belief that this universe is all about us, as well as that we're graded according to how much stuff we accumulate, how much we accomplish, and how many merit badges we manage to secure. That is, our acquisitions, achievements, and reputations are of primary significance.

The next three components of our ego portfolio are organized around the desire to stand out as original, unique, and different from everyone and everything else in the universe.

4. "I Am Separate from Everyone Else"

In the ego sense, Ambition wants us to believe that we're the only one who matters. If we're well indoctrinated in this ego belief, it's very difficult to consider the idea of Earth existing without us, or of Earth having a reason to be here in the first place! The key word in these final three components of ego's inventory is *separation.*

If we believe that we're separate and distinct from everyone else, we fulfill the false self's program. But recall that we emerged from nonbeing, characterized by oneness. Allow this statement by Thomas Merton to settle within you: "We are already one. But we imagine that we are not. And what we have to recover is our original unity." Merton's words have the ring of truth, and they deny ego's insistent edict of separation.

Ego insists on separation because that's how it undermines allegiance to the authentic self. When we recognize and respect our connectedness to each other; the air we breathe, the water we drink, and the sun we rely on; and, most significantly, the invisible Source we're animated by, the ego can return to its rightful space.

Ramana Maharshi's contention that "there are no others" is deliciously thought provoking and, for me, essentially puts ego completely out of business. Ego survives and thrives on the basis of our belief in our separation from others. Separation serves as a motivating factor in our journey of ambition in that it gets us to exercise our comparison mentality with thoughts such as: *I'm prettier, smarter, more talented, a better performer,* and on and on. With this attitude firmly entrenched, we pursue the business of proving our superiority in relation to others. If we're aware that there's no separation—no others—we don't need to prove our superiority.

By contrast, when our connectedness to others dominates our beliefs, we don't need to defeat anyone, fight for what we identify as our rights, wage war, take advantage of others, or continually try to be someone we think of as a winner. Instead, seeing the unfolding of God in everyone means that there's no conflict, since we see ourselves in others. We understand the wisdom in this observation: *When you judge other people, you do not define them; rather, you define yourself as someone who needs to judge.* We're unable to grasp the idea of "enemy," and consequently unable to participate in killing or waging war on any member of humankind. As the Native Americans love to say, "No tree has branches so foolish as to fight among themselves."

Studying the history of humanity reveals that we've been at war with each of the branches on the same tree for more than 95 percent of recorded history. This is the result of ego convincing us that we're separate and need to fight, control, and vanquish "others" who live across the river, speak a different language, practice a different religion, or have different cultural attitudes. Competitiveness, fighting, rip-offs, hatred, and conflicts of all descriptions stem from the false self the ego creates when we allow it to convince us that we must preserve the illusion of our separateness.

Ambition is so often a drive to excel by judging ourselves as superior to "them." The reality is, *they* are us in disguise as *them*. Instead of noticing our oneness, we focus on the differentness that ego perpetrates. As Lao-tzu relates in the Tao Te Ching:

There is no greater loss
Than feeling: "I have an enemy,"
For when "I" and "enemy" co-exist
My treasure becomes obscured.

The treasure is the universal unifying force that is in all things: the all-knowing Tao.

Regarding the ego's need to believe in separateness, the Upanishads say, "When to a man who understands, the Self has become all things, what sorrow, what trouble can there be to him who once beheld that unity?" This is illustrated in the film *The Shift*. The businessman, Chad, is such a believer in his separateness that he runs his company with no concern for its impact on others or the environment. Toward the end of the film, however, he begins to notice the spirit in which Joe, the owner of the resort Chad and his wife are staying in, serves others. As Chad writes a sizable check to donate to the charity House of Promise and Hope, his smile tells us that he's recognized there's more to life than making money at the expense of others.

5. "I Am Separate from What's Missing in My Life"

An ancient tale relates the story of a young boy who lived in a small village. This boy had qualities of an avatar, and people were healed by being in his presence. Many villagers spoke of his ability to bilocate, to be seen in two different places at precisely the same instant. His countenance was peaceful, and he radiated tranquility. The elders of the tribe beseeched this young avatar to tell them the secrets of God and the universe. One of them pleaded, "I will give you an orange if you will tell me where God is." The young saint responded without hesitation, "I will give you two oranges right now if you can tell me where God *isn't*."

The fifth component of ego, our false self, refuses to believe that there's no place that God is not. (*God* is the word I use here in reference to the creative Source responsible for all of creation.) Ego has a vested interest in our believing that there are things missing in our life. It insists that we're not connected to an invisible creative Source because it gets its identity by edging God out. If we start believing that we're permanently attached to God, ego's reason for existence disappears. If there's no place that God is not, then God is in each of us, as well as in everything that our senses interpret as missing from our life. This means that in some invisible manner, we're connected to everything we perceive to be missing. The question might then be, how do we manifest the things we desire that appear to be unavailable? The answer is to realign ourselves in a way that allows what we seek to spiritually harmonize with us.

But ego wants us to strive, set goals, believe in shortages, compete with all of the other individuals who are also searching for the same missing stuff—even fight for it—and ultimately emerge a discontent searcher. Why discontent? Because ego's method doesn't permit arriving in the sense of living peacefully and contentedly in the precious present moment. Ego's method is to be ambitious in the sense of searching, striving, and always desiring more. Ego utilizes its strength to encourage us to maintain the status of being an ambitious person.

Ego defines Ambition as striving to be better than everyone else, winning at all costs, accumulating more stuff, and being seen by others as brilliantly successful. Obviously, ego needs us to reject any idea of being connected in oneness to all that exists in the world. We must instead prove our alignment with Ambition by having lofty goals and objectives. The bigger the goals, the more status we acquire as ambitious men and women. And the more we believe that our goals and plans must be big, the more we're aware of what's missing.

Ego shouts, "Who you are is insufficient! Can't you see that you don't have enough stuff? Your means for acquiring all of the stuff you need to prove your worthiness is in short supply. If you don't go after it, someone else will get there first! Then you'll have to compete with them for the limited amount that's out there!" These messages keep us from living our life from our authentic self's perspective.

Our real self knows that we don't need one more thing in order to be worthy, and that believing we do need anything else in order to be happy could be a definition of insanity. It also knows that there are no shortages in this universe. But ego is terrified of our belief that abundance and contentment are readily available. Ego needs us to be convinced that Ambition is a healthy way to assuage our discontent with all the things that are missing in our life. But we'll never completely erase that discontent! Ambition in this ego sense can mean spending a lifetime striving to get someplace else, which will almost instantly need to be upgraded to something else that's missing. This rat race continues, energized by the idea that there's never enough.

However, we have the power to eliminate ego's insane ideology of striving, and instead live in a state of contentment. In the process, our connectedness to everyone and everything will be clarified. Rather than strive for what we perceive to be missing, and then be unable to find contentment, we can relax in harmony with our Source of being. Then there's no need to edge God out, since we're resting in oneness. There's no need for that troublesome ego.

It feels to me like logic would then dictate the following:

God (Spirit or Tao) is everywhere.
Therefore, God is in me.
God is in everything I perceive to be missing.
Conclusion: I am connected by Spirit to every-
thing I view as missing.
Suggested action: Align with Spirit and see
that what appeared to be missing begins to
show up.

The naturalist John Muir described this phe-
nomenon like this: "When we try to pick out
anything by itself, we find it hitched to everything else in the Universe." We simply need
to pay attention to this fundamental truth,
and ignore ego's insistence that we must strive
hard to get what we want.

6. "I Am Separate from God"

In this sixth component, the *ego* acronym continues to effectively describe our actions of
edging God out by believing that we're not
the same as what we come from. The God
essence and our worldly self remain ensconced

in distinct and separate compartments. Ego is terrified that we'll believe we're a piece of God. Its leadership position is doomed if we truly realize our Godness. Naturally, one of ego's primary functions is to keep us believing that we're two very distinct and separate entities.

The collective consciousness of humanity painfully and unnecessarily influences us by believing in, and behaving like, an ego-designed god. A few of the attributes of this ego-designed deity are that it plays favorites, craves opulence, promotes killing and warfare in its name, accepts indulgences for special favors, punishes bad behavior, and needs to be avenged. These and many other attitudes illustrate a god created by the illusions of the collective ego.

Throughout history, this ego-designed, human-made creator has been characterized as separate from us. Who among us hasn't heard of God portrayed as a white dead male with a long flowing beard, floating around the heavens with supernatural powers, watching over us like a cosmic bellboy who will answer our prayers sometimes, depending on His whims and whether we've obeyed His rules? This entity is viewed not as an all-giving Divine source, but rather as a temperamental superpower who withholds His ability to solve our problems, or heals our diseases depending on whether He's in the mood to grant us special dispensation. This is a creator of the ego, invented by ego and dedicated to serving ego's demands. This is a creator who must, by virtue of its own ego, be separate from the subjects it must watch over, control, and punish when necessary.

What does it take to shift out of this detrimental belief system? Certainly, scorching the ego, as Ramana Maharshi suggests in the quote that opens this chapter, is symbolically appealing. In the film *The Shift,* I suggest thinking of our relationship to God or the great Tao by imagining the ocean as symbolic of God, and ourselves symbolized by a small glass of water from the ocean. If asked what's in the glass, we'd say, "A glass of God. It's not as big or as strong, but it's a glass of God." If we empty the glass of water on the sidewalk, we'd see it disappear as it vaporized. Ultimately, it would return to its source. While the ocean water is in the glass, separate from its source, it lacks the power of the ocean. But when it rejoins its source, it is once again part of the powerful ocean. That water on the sidewalk having lost its connection to its source is a symbol of ego.

■ ■ ■

In the second half of this book, we'll discover how to maintain our connection to Source and our authentic self in form in this world. We will learn how to shift from the Ambition of ego and its inevitable evaporation of power to the oneness of joyous Meaning, where we realize that we are so much more than our possessions, accomplishments, and reputations. The shift to Meaning eliminates our feelings of separateness, and illuminates our spiritual connectedness.

■ ■ ■ ■ ■

CHAPTER THREE
TO ...

"Thoroughly unprepared, we take the step into the afternoon of life; worse still, we take this step with the false assumption that our truths and ideals will serve us as hitherto. But we cannot live the afternoon of life according to the programme of life's morning; for what was great in the morning will be little at evening, and what in the morning was true will at evening have become a lie."

— from *The Stages of Life*, by Carl Jung[1]

The title of this chapter signifies the step we take *away* from the demands of the ego (the false self that thrives on Ambition) *toward* the authentic self (which is nourished by, and nourishes, purpose). Jung uses the morning of life as a metaphor to illustrate that early on, we allow ego to be the dominant influence. Yet there comes a time for everyone when ego's influence is so inauthentic and inappropriate as to be a lie.

Carl Jung is telling us that all of the "truths and ideals" we learn during the years of constructing a belief in the false self are ineffectual guides for the afternoon and evening of life. The shift starts between the so-called morning and afternoon, when we begin yearning to find "something more" in our existence. We then begin the move to a life that's governed by our soul's call for something more—something purposeful—rather than the meager illusory offerings of the ego. Jung further warns us that ego's guidance is ultimately false when applied to the afternoon and evening metaphor.

This chapter explores altering the direction that ego wants us to take, by making a U-turn back to our "Fromness." Still very much alive, we simply set out on the path to fulfilling our dharma—the Meaning of our life. The U-turn is a shift from Ambition back to our place of origination to fulfill the promise of the after-noon and evening of our life. That promise is a life saturated with purpose.

Making the U-turn

The *direction* we take in life is far more sig-nificant than the *place* ego parks us in, in the present moment. For example, inquiring about what direction we're headed is more valuable than focusing on how much we weigh or when we had our last cigarette. Making a commit-ment to change a self-sabotaging way of life is making a commitment to change direc-tion, and then we head toward weight loss or addiction control. Heading toward something more purposeful and meaningful is even more significant.

If we persistently listen to the demands of ego, we move away from our Source of being. The ego insists on pursuing more: more stuff, accomplishments, status, triumphs, and money. *More* is the mantra of the ego, fueling endless striving with a false promise of eventually arriving. However, every assured arrival point is seductively transformed to a desire to strive for even more, unless we choose to make a shift in the direction our life is taking. The shift begins in the process of halting the momentum and self-importance of the ego, but then we must proceed with the work of derailing and rerouting it in the opposite direction. This doesn't mean we lose our drive; rather, it signifies that our drive is realigned with a life based on experiencing Meaning and feeling purposeful.

Ambition is now fueled by our Source of being, and it's vibrating at a higher frequency than the false self fueled by ego. Returning to our natural Source, the "Fromness" I described earlier as our origination point puts us on track to a way of life that supports the potential wholeness that we are.

Here are some of the signposts of our readiness to make the U-turn From Ambition To Meaning:

— **Ego's repetitious insistence to do and have more becomes less attractive.** Instead, we begin to notice an interest in where we're headed *To*. (Although this may be a grammatically incorrect construction, it's a necessary emphasis in light of the title of this chapter.) Gradually, we may hear a part of ourselves that whispers questions such as: "Is this all there is?" "What's it all about?" and "What's the point?" We begin questioning the ego part of us that seems to be in charge, telling us that life is about what we do and what we have. We begin shifting our attention to our Source, which is saying quite the opposite.

The Tao Te Ching instructs us to let go of everything, to remove our attachments. This part of the 81st verse particularly speaks to challenging ego's voice:

> *Sages do not accumulate anything*
> *but give everything to others;*
> *having more, the more they give.*

We notice that life begins to take a different direction when we get on track, headed back home in this metaphorical sense. We begin to understand that we have more by detaching from the need to acquire and accumulate. This very point is underscored in my movie, when Chad the CEO detaches from his desire to acquire as he writes out his donation check to the House of Hope and Promise. This is followed by a scene in which he gives his wife wild roses, which symbolize his decision to change his life direction.

Changing direction from a less-than-authentic existence to an authentic one doesn't mean that we're no longer able to attract abundance and prosperity, or that we lose our desire to be productive. It *does* mean that we feel the natural bliss of being tuned in to our wholeness.

— **We begin to shift from doing more to doing less.** Our Source of being encourages us to be like the Tao and do less. Lao-tzu states that by doing nothing, everything is done. Likewise, Jesus tells us, "Look at the birds of the air, for they neither sow nor reap nor gather into barns; yet your heavenly Father feeds them" (Matthew 6:26). This shift is away from the Ambition of "gaining the whole world," which Jesus refers to when he asks, "For what will it profit a man if he gains the whole world, and loses his own soul?" (Mark 8:36).

On the journey of To—that is, back to our original nature—we do more of what the recovery movement teaches in that we "let go and let God." Without pressuring ourselves to achieve at all costs, we attain the wondrous position of accomplishing more, and we ultimately feel more significance in our life.

— **We begin to shun the spotlight and function more from the shadows.** Our Source of being says that humility should be our primary focus. But for years, ego has been effectively convincing us that we must focus on acquiring a reputation for being an ambitious person. In the shift From Ambition To Meaning, we absorb the truth of the Tao and find ourselves attracted to statements such as this one, from verse 73: "It is heaven's way to conquer without striving." Our desire for accolades shifts to the opposite of ego's edicts. Jesus similarly speaks in opposition to the ego when he states, "For he who is least among you all—he is the greatest" (Luke 9:48). Imagine the difficulty ego has when we begin practicing this kind of radical humility!

Ego thrives on the approval of others and the accolades that come our way, so it isn't surprising that we learn to adopt an approval-seeking lifestyle. We've sought approval since we were toddlers. As we reverse our direction and begin diminishing our self importance, however, we become independent of the good or bad opinions of others.

— **A belief in unity replaces our belief in separation.** Ego has long insisted that we're separate from everyone else and therefore special. The obstinate conviction in separateness has meant that we constantly compare ourselves with each other and compete for what we desire—we've learned to fight and even go to war if necessary to sustain that notion. Conflict is a necessary part of ego's belief in separation, and the need to dominate and destroy others is all part and parcel of this mind-set.

As we head back to our "Fromness," a sense of oneness begins replacing separateness. Our Source of being tells us that we're all connected, so we start feeling less competitive—our desire to dominate is replaced by compassion, and controlling others is no longer appealing. The language of Spirit instructs us, in the language of the Tao Te Ching, to "never think of conquering others by force. Whatever strains with force will soon decay. It is not attuned to the Way." All conflicts, be they in our personal life or the larger world, stem from heading away from our Source of being. Thanks to its belief in separation, the ego steers us toward force rather than empowerment. The words of Jesus are once again in harmony with the ancient Tao: "Blessed are the peacemakers, for they will be called children of God." (Matthew 5:9).

One of the characters in *The Shift* is completely tuned in to his oneness with others. His name is Joe, and it's initially unclear whether he's a janitor, gardener, or perhaps a waiter. But it's obvious that his ego is unpretentious; he functions in a calm, sensitive, and sincerely joyful manner in service to all the guests at the resort. Meaning and purpose have replaced any need for Ambition and control for Joe. Throughout the film, he illustrates the kind of behavior that occurs when we are aware of the oneness that unites us.

— We begin realizing that we're connected in Spirit to everything we perceive to be missing from our life. During the morning of life, ego has insisted that we're separate from everything that's missing in our life, and that we must chase our desires. It pushes us to strive, struggle, fight, work hard, and apply a determinedly ambitious approach to life—it insists that this is how we succeed in being considered successful by our peers. Convinced that we're separate, we conclude that what's missing is due to our separateness. Yet we come from a oneness where there is no such thing. Our Source of being gently reminds us that we are connected to everything, so we must be connected to what we think is missing.

This chapter emphasizes that we shift or move back *To* something ego is unfamiliar with. The Tao Te Ching reminds us that the great Tao is omnipresent, which means that there's no place it is not. And Jesus proclaims: "The kingdom of God is among you" (Luke 17:21). Ego, on the other hand, defines separateness as separation from everything we can't grasp with our senses.

When we head back in the direction of where we reconnect to our Source of being, the journey is typified by an alignment in which we think and act like the Tao that flows everywhere. The Tao that "covers all creatures like the sky, but does not dominate them. All things return to it as their home, but it does not lord it over them." As we move in this direction, there's no possibility of shortage or lack. We become content and grateful for all that we have.

— **We begin trusting the wisdom that created us.** Ego constantly dissuades us from believing in our Divinity, insisting that we're separate from God. Our Source of being, however, tells us that we're an inseparable piece of God. If we believe as Jesus taught, that "I and the Father are one" (John 10:30), then there would be no need for the ego.

As we embark on our return trip, we see the folly of continuing to believe that our Source of being could ever be separate from us. We know that we're not distinct, fearful creatures who are dependent on a moody and sometimes malevolent god for our sustenance. We begin to see ourselves as Lao-tzu describes: "Carrying body and soul and embracing the one." We abandon the material ego focus and can no longer see ourselves as separate from God.

As we become one with our Source, we begin the realignment process, thinking and contemplating more like God. We gain the wisdom necessary to understand these words written by Thomas Troward: "If you contemplate with thoughts that match originating Spirit, you have the same power as originating Spirit." This idea is anathema to the ego. But the wholeness, the oneness, that we truly are, is revealed as we begin trusting the wisdom that created us.

What to Expect as We Change the Direction of Our Life

As with anything new, shifting from the morning of life into the afternoon and then evening will produce some surprising situations. This new direction, From Ambition To Meaning, is often accompanied by an unexpected event.

I've found that every spiritual advance I've made was preceded by some sort of a fall—in fact, it's almost a universal law that a fall of some kind precedes a major shift. A fall can be an embarrassing event that reveals the exaggerated influence ego has been allowed to play in one's life, which certainly happened to me when I was prompted to end my association with alcohol. Other kinds of falls may involve an accident, a fire that destroys all the stuff we've worked so hard to accumulate, an illness, a failed relationship, a death or injury that causes deep sorrow, an abandonment, a serious addiction, a business failure, a bankruptcy, or the like. These low points actually provide the energy needed to make a shift in direction away from an ego-driven life to one full of purpose.

When I was in high school, I was the high jumper on the boys' track team. In order to propel myself over the bar, I'd approach the high-jump pit and get down as low as I could. In the process of getting down so low, I was creating the position necessary to propel myself high enough to sail over the bar. For me, this is symbolic of what happens preceding a shift: in a metaphorical sense, getting down can mean that we're low enough to access the energy needed to change life direction.

Every fall has within it the potential to move us to a higher place. It may be necessary to get down and dirty in the dark night of the soul in order to free ourselves from the grip of a well-established ego. "Hidden in all misfortune is good fortune" is a Tao concept that seems to support the value of those times in life when we've experienced a fall. Without that particular misfortune, good fortune is unavailable.

Elisabeth Kübler-Ross puts these events in the category of nature's work: "Should you shield the canyons from the windstorms, you would never see the beauty of their carvings."[2] The windstorms of life are potentially meaningful events, and we can use them to propel ourselves to higher places. In fact, it is my contention that the bigger the purpose we signed up for in life, the bigger and harder the falls we encounter will be.

A mild heart attack helped me become more caring toward the suffering of others. Being in a series of foster homes taught me self-reliance as a young boy, which consequently led me to become a teacher of self-reliance. A deeply painful separation from my wife allowed me to write from a more compassionate heart. I came here to accomplish big things, you see; therefore, I am not at all surprised when the challenges and the falls come in big doses. In fact, I now feel that any big challenge is an opportunity to grow to a higher spiritual level, where gratitude gradually replaces remorse.

I absolutely love this Rumi observation, which reveals what I consider to be an essential truth:

> *The spiritual path wrecks the body*
> *and afterwards restores it to health.*
> *It destroys the house to unearth the treasure*
> *and with that treasure builds it better than*
> *before.*[3]

This has been my experience as I look back at how I made a change in direction and shifted From Ambition To Meaning. All of the falls unearthed a treasure in me that wouldn't have been usable had my "house" not been destroyed. Those windstorms of life helped carve the body of work that millions of readers and listeners appreciate.

Each of the characters in the movie *The Shift* experiences some "ego unearthing" preceding their own shift to a more meaningful life. David the filmmaker almost collapses as he is dealt a blow that destroys his visions of success. Chad the CEO faces the wrath of his pregnant wife, risking his marriage over his ego's stance. And then there's Quinn and Jason, a couple with two young boys—Jason grapples with the issue of becoming a temporary homemaker in order to assist Quinn in fulfilling her dharma as an artist. The fact is that all of these falls, minor or catastrophic, are experiences that can be tipping points that elevate these individuals' consciousness to a place where significance and purpose are the touchstones of their lives.

Each of the components of ego make entirely different demands than our Source of being does. Spirit calls us home to a perfect alignment with our Creator; ego is moving at high speed in the opposite direction. We must get better acquainted with Spirit if we wish to make a U-turn while we're still alive . . . and fully experience the afternoon of life.

Preparing to Make the U-turn

The Bhagavad Gita tells us: "We are born into the world of nature; our second birth is into the world of Spirit."[4] Taming the influence of the ego is the beginning of that second birth. By taming the ego, we elicit the support and assistance of our originating Spirit, and we come to notice synchronicities happening in our life. The people we need appear, circumstances come together in a way that assists us on our dharma path, financing becomes available that was never there before, and so on.

In the words of Patanjali, "Dormant forces, faculties, and talents come alive, and you discover yourself to be a greater person by far than you ever dreamed yourself to be." This great Hindu philosopher is referring to what happens when we move into a spiritual mindset, rather than an ego-dominated one: that which previously appeared to be nonexistent suddenly comes alive. This is the result of reversing the direction of life and knowing where we are headed *To* (the title of this chapter).

The most important thing we can do to defuse the influence of ego is to proclaim ourselves *ready!* Remember the ancient saying that instructs: "When the student is ready, the teacher will appear." The teachers and teachings are always there, throughout the entire span of our life. But when ego is running things, those teachers go unnoticed. Once we truly acknowledge our readiness to live a life on purpose and filled with meaning, there's very little to do. We begin living in a different world than we experience in our ego-directed persona. As I've written and said many times: *When we change the way we look at things, the things we look at change.*

Briefly summarized, here's what happens when ego does a U-turn and heads in the direction of our place of origination:

The 7-Step Summary of Our U-turn

1. We shift to personal empowerment. Our ego self has always focused on external power. As we move toward Spirit, though, we replace ego's need to influence external situations or other people with a preference for personal empowerment. We stop fighting ego's endless battles and instead shift to Meaning. We do this through conscious compassionate curiosity, and caring first and foremost for our inner self. Noninterference becomes a higher priority than being right or dominating others.

2. We see ourselves connected to everyone. Ego feels separate and distinct from others, a being unto itself. As we move back to Spirit, we recognize our connectedness. The essence of living a life on purpose is to think like God thinks, and the creative Source of all life is just that—responsible for all life. We all share the same Source and have the same destiny. Seeing ourselves as a part of everyone eliminates the need to compete with anyone.

3. We are motivated by ethics, serenity, and quality of life. Ego is motivated by external achievement, performance, and acquisitions. As we move back to Spirit, we shift our focus to internal pursuits. Our preparation for living a life of purpose involves a major shift in attitude in the direction of feeling peaceful, being honest, and assisting others.

4. We shift to the possibility, even the expectation, of miracles being a part of life. As we move toward originating Spirit, ego's investment in a scientific cause-and-effect interpretation of life is diluted. We acknowledge the presence of the mysterious and unfathomable, and we relinquish skepticism by relying less on our senses and much more on our intuitive knowing.

5. We pursue a meditation practice. Ego eschews the practice of meditation and often labels it as a waste of time—or even worse, lunacy. Shifting to our Source of being leads us to seek silence to consciously contact God as a natural component of a meaningful life.

6. We begin to recognize ourselves in nature's beauty and intricacy. Ego's interest in contemplating the beauty of nature is minimal. When we journey back in the direction of Spirit, our interest in the miracles that appear in the natural world is endless. Out of this grows our preference to live in harmony with this universe, rather than to exert influence and power over it.

7. We are less judgmental, and we easily understand and forgive. Ego is rather adamant about the importance of seeking revenge. Shifting to Source causes us to enjoy opportunities to practice forgiveness. Pursuing and achieving vengeance, retaliation, and reprisal prevent us from feeling purposeful and living a life of Meaning. We become truly sensitive to the edict that we don't define others by our judgments; we are simply defining ourselves as people who need to judge.

■   ■   ■

These 7 distinctions between ego's ambitions and a desire to live a life of meaning could easily be extended to 70 times 7. Essentially, the process of shifting to Meaning involves reconsidering our role in this magnificent, mysterious universe from a spiritual perspective. We recognize our longing for more significance and purpose, and realize that ego isn't capable of fulfilling that yearning.

Whether personally articulated or not, we cannot achieve authenticity from the false self, which is ego.

This is entertainingly illustrated by the personal stories of David, Chad, and Quinn in the movie version of *The Shift*. We see them in their frustration of endlessly *striving*, which is the way of Ambition in an ego-dominated life, and watch them as they shift to Meaning and consequently discover the joy of *arriving*. In the film, ego loses its influence as each of these characters tires of continually striving and never arriving.

A signal that the *To* dimension of the shift is upon us is that we, like the film's three central characters, begin to tire of the angst of continually striving and never arriving. Our view of our world changes as we permit quantum moments to get, and then hold, our attention.

Quantum Moments Can Turn Life Upside Down

I discuss quantum moments in the film, along with the fact that they've been reported by thousands of people who have experienced a shift in their awareness about life. These people have made the move from an ego-driven life perspective to a spiritually balanced one, and have become more authentic beings.

There are four qualities that help us recognize a quantum moment, the kind with the potential to introduce us to our authentic self. In their book, *Quantum Change: When Epiphanies and Sudden Insights Transform Ordinary Lives,* authors William R. Miller and Janet C'de Baca state that *"quantum change is a vivid, surprising, benevolent, and enduring personal transformation."* (Please note that the italics are courtesy of the authors of *Quantum Change.*)

What follows is how *I* view those four qualities—in a slightly different order—in relation to our making the shift From Ambition To Meaning:

1. Surprising! It might sound contradictory to plan on being surprised, but everyone reports that quantum moments are unexpected, uninvited, and unforeseen. This is when synchronicity and serendipity collaborate to astound us.

It's as if we surrender and let ourselves be lived by life. We become the student who is ready, and the teacher does in fact appear. However, this is generally preceded by a fall.

Earlier in this chapter I wrote about the falls that we often take prior to any kind of spiritual advance. The universe seems to work in this way, and I could recount many examples from my own life. As I mentioned previously, my final decision to live an alcohol-free life involved a quantum moment that totally surprised me.

On that particular day, I was awakened at 4:07 A.M. to a voice, a faint smell of roses in the room, and an overwhelming feeling of being in the presence of Divine energy. There appeared to be a slight breeze in my enclosed bedroom, and while I was transfixed and feeling a gooseflesh sensation throughout my body, I was also stunned by what was happening in the moment. The voice told me that I was through with alcohol and that it would be easy to give it up.

It's now two decades later, and I can report with total honesty that what I was told was 100 percent true: I've never been tempted to include alcohol in my life again. This was a total surprise to me. Yet as I've shifted in the direction of Spirit, over the years, I've had *many* of these surprises, which attracted my attention and led me to greater spiritual consciousness.

2. Vivid! These quantum moments that turn life upside down are also characterized as being extremely intense. Even to this day, I can recall every detail of that spectacular quantum moment that occurred when I gave up alcohol. The sheets on the bed, the clothes hanging over the top of my closet door, a little cartoon taped to a mirror above my dresser, the container of coins on the floor, the color of the walls, a scratch mark on my headboard . . . everything is as vivid to me today as it was more than 20 years ago. It seems to me that when Spirit calls, it creates an exclamation point to emphasize the entire episode. There's a vividness that stays with us forever.

3. Benevolent! The third quality of these quantum moments is that they're benevolent.

For example, the early-morning adventure I just related was one of the most peaceful and blissful times I've ever experienced. The ease that embraced me was like being cradled in the arms of a truly loving and generous Creator. For years I'd had thoughts about my dependency on a few beers every evening. I'd try to think back to a day when I hadn't had a beer in the evening and couldn't recall a day in the previous decade or possibly more. I told myself it wasn't a dependency because I never got drunk or put myself or anyone else in danger by driving under the influence.

However, in my inner place of truth, I knew that I was dependent on this beer-drinking activity and that it was interfering in my life in potentially damaging ways. Yet I still persisted—that is, until my fall and the quantum moment. To this day, I count that early-morning encounter with whatever it was as one of the most rapturous and serene moments of my life. The experience of the benevolence of a quantum moment shifted me to a totally new world where Meaning replaced the Ambition of the ego.

4. Enduring! The fourth quality of a quantum moment is that it never goes away. The enduring truth from my example is that I'm in my third decade of total abstinence. Had I continued on my same beer-drinking path, I quite likely wouldn't have lived long enough to write what I'm relating to you now.

When we're in the process of turning our life around to reflect Meaning rather than ego's Ambition, we will have a quantum moment that's surprising, vivid, benevolent, and enduring. That moment will be burned into our consciousness in a vivid picture that won't be forgotten. I've heard it described as being like a warm shower running inside yourself whose gracious imprint endures into infinity.

How Life Changes after a Quantum-Moment Experience

My earliest books focus almost exclusively on psychological tools to help readers employ effective commonsense approaches to problems. There are no references to God or a higher self in the first 15 or so years of my publishing history. Today, my values and my writing reflect the shift From Ambition To Meaning that took place later in my life and writing career. Had I attempted to live the afternoon of my life according to the program of my life's morning, I would have been living a lie, as Carl Jung points out in the last sentence of the quotation that opens this chapter.

Prior to those quantum moments, my life was shaped much more extensively by my ego. I probably would have responded like the men and women who participated in the studies that are reported in *Quantum Change:* after asking the individuals to define what effect their quantum-moment experiences had on their lives, the authors concluded that the "person's value system was often turned upside down."

The top-five values for men before their quantum moment were: *wealth, adventure, achievement, pleasure,* and *being respected.* I interpret these as the "morning" values, prior to the shift From Ambition To Meaning. There's no judgment intended here—these qualities are simply what ego has been taught to believe is important and necessary for success.

Early in life, men learn that their job is to make money and their worth depends on how much money they've accumulated. Males who grow to adulthood in a society that empha-sizes ego consistently report similar shared values. A man believes that he must amass wealth, have adventure, achieve at all costs, and seek pleasure by making himself the most important person in all respects, especially regarding intimacy. *Me first. As long as I feel pleasure, everything is fine.* And the need to be respected at all costs is a key reason for the conflicts that rage in our male-dominated, war-ravaged world.

What these same men (and I include myself with them) report as prime values after a quan-tum moment is one of the main messages of *The Shift.* The top priority for these men was a value that didn't appear anywhere on the list when they were in the morning of their lives: spirituality. That's right—after a move toward the afternoon of life, spirituality tops the list.

In fact, *Quantum Change* reports that the five most valued characteristics with that original group of men were now: *spirituality, personal peace, family, God's will,* and *honesty*. It's easy to understand why a quantum moment would be seen as turning life upside down! This is a complete shift away from the pleadings of the ego and back home to desiring a God-realized life of peace, family, love, and personal honesty.

For women, the shift away from the morning's ego-driven messages is every bit as fascinating. When asked to prioritize their values pre-quantum moment, their number one value was *family*. This isn't surprising because women have been programmed to believe that being a mother/daughter/wife supersedes all else. This isn't meant to denigrate the female roles of mother, daughter, sister, grandmother, and so on; rather, I mean to give credence to the fact that there's more to being a woman than being someone else's walking to-do list. Every woman has a dharma. Yet quite often, she relegates her personal dharma to an unimportant status compared to her family roles.

The next pre-quantum highest values were: *independence, career, fitting in,* and *attractiveness.* This attitude is dramatically characterized in the movie when Sarah describes the conflicts women experience. They want to be good mothers, yet independence and a career are at the top of their list of values. Furthermore, prior to a quantum experience, they rank "fitting in" and "being attractive" as very high priorities. But after making the shift into the afternoon of life, which is frequently aided by a surprising quantum-moment experience, women report that their values take on an entirely new flavor.

According to *Quantum Change, personal growth* topped the list in women's post-quantum questioning, followed by *self-esteem, spirituality, happiness,* and *generosity*—five things that did not even make the list in the morning of women's lives. As the females in the studies became more conscious of their spiritual nature, their concept of themselves began to shift. Previously, things like spirituality and self-esteem were not considered to be important values. But after their quantum moments, they were given a totally new set of values and propelled in a new direction: the purposeful afternoon of life.

I commend William R. Miller and Janet C'de Baca for their groundbreaking research, and I highly recommend that you check out their book. I guarantee that you will find it as fascinating as I do.

■   ■   ■

It's fitting to end this chapter titled "To," which signifies the new direction of our lives when we're open to the shift, with the final words from Carl Jung's quotation at the opening of this chapter: "for what was great in the morning will be little at evening, and what in the morning was true will at evening have become a lie."

Our life, and the lives of those we impact, will be devoid of any lies when we shed our false self and shift into the afternoon and evening. This is the subject of the next and final chapter, titled "Meaning."

■   ■   ■   ■   ■

CHAPTER FOUR
MEANING ...

"Life is not meaningful . . .
unless it is serving an end beyond itself;
unless it is of value to someone else."

— Abraham Joshua Heschel

"The one possible way of giving meaning
to [man's] existence is that of raising his
natural relation to the world to a spiritual one."

— Albert Schweitzer

Here we are at the end, which ironically turns
out to be identical to the place from which
we originated. Our goal in this journey From

Ambition To Meaning has been to return to the place from which we originated, and in the words of T. S. Eliot, "know the place for the first time."

We came from a placeless place of purpose and significance. At birth we took on a false self known as ego, and we spent a period of our life endeavoring to satisfy its ambitious cravings. Then we made a shift in direction and began heading back home. Here we are in the meaningful afternoon of life, the place where, to paraphrase the Emmanuel quote earlier in the book:

Our mind doesn't know the way,
Our heart has already been there,
And our soul never left.
Welcome home!

Having arrived home, each breath we take is an expression of our life purpose. We no longer struggle to win; gain the approval of others; meet expectations others had for us; fulfill someone else's idea of our dharma; or acquire, achieve, or hoard. We let go of conflict, certainty, being right, fighting, dominating, vanquishing, and feeling superior. All of this ego stuff loses its power and attraction when we arrive home, where Meaning welcomes us.

Many years ago, after a conversation with my friend Ram Dass, I wrote these words: *All of my life I wanted to be somebody. Now I finally am somebody—but it isn't me.* I strove to become that somebody whom everyone admired for all of his ego strengths, vast accomplishments, accumulation of wealth, and houseful of merit badges . . . yet I ultimately came to realize that it wasn't me. The components of the ego were well established, but I had miles to go before I could truly say, "I'm living out my dharma. I am on purpose, and my life means something."

Abraham Heschel's quote at the beginning of this chapter explains what was missing. He notes that meaningfulness is unavailable unless one's life is "serving an end beyond itself; unless it is of value to someone else." That somebody I wanted to be—who, by all accounts, I had actually become—wasn't the authentic me. I came into this world, just like you and everyone else, with nothing (that is, no things). I will leave this world the same way, with nothing. My conclusion? Since we don't get to keep anything we accomplish or accumulate, the only thing we can do with our life is to give it away.

Albert Schweitzer, a man I so admire, explains in the second quote that opens this chapter that the way to give Meaning to life is to raise our consciousness to a spiritual awareness, rather than a material one. This means learning to think like God thinks, which I emphasize throughout this book and in my movie. *This* is the big shift: away from ego and back to the oneness of Spirit, while staying alive yet dead to the false self.

Preparing for a Life of Meaning

How do we live our lives in this egoless place of home? As you might suspect, Lao-tzu offers us a few clues on how this is accomplished.

First, he notes what is necessary to feel the sense of heaven on Earth referred to as "immortality":

> *The mystical techniques for achieving*
> *immortality are*
> *revealed only to those who have*
> *dissolved all ties to*
> *the gross worldly realm of duality,*
> *conflict, and dogma.*
> *As long as your shallow worldly*
> *ambitions exist,*
> *the door will not open.*[1]

If we can't at least get this process started, in other words, we're left with the frustrations of ego, and the door to immortality simply won't open. To live a life of Meaning, we're required to do a radical ego-ectomy and dissolve our ties to what Lao-tzu calls "the world of the 10,000 things." As he advises:

> *When you succeed in connecting your*
> *energy with the divine realm through*
> *high awareness and the practice of*
> *undiscriminating virtue, the transmission of*
> *the ultimate subtle truths will follow.*[2]

As we dissolve our ties to the material world and simultaneously connect to the Divine realm, we have the opportunity to receive guidance from beyond ourselves. We know then what a life of purpose and significance feels like on a daily basis. It is never about ego.

Lao-tzu knew this truth 2,500 years ago, and Jesus reminded us of it 500 years later in the teachings of the New Testament: A life full of Meaning celebrates the perfection of ourselves and nature—we are in harmony with everyone and everything around us. Yet this harmonious state can't be accomplished when we adopt the characteristics of ego. To be able to enter a life of Spirit and purpose, we have to give our life away. This is a concept that ego will ridicule, even working overtime to convince us that it will have disastrous consequences.

■   ■   ■

Authentic self wonders: *How may I serve?* Ego's attitude, on the other hand, is: *Gimme, gimme, gimme—I need more, and I can never be satisfied.* When we align with ego's voice, the universe provides experiences that match the *Gimme, gimme, gimme* energy. It may not seem obvious at first, but if we pay attention, it's quite clear that this energy creates pressure, anxiety, and stress. Why? Because allying with ego means that we've chosen to live in a demanding environment. We simply haven't realized that we have a choice to join forces with our authentic ideals and live in a nondemanding environment. The Law of Attraction works either way!

The more we demand from the universe, the more is demanded of us. The more we give away, the more is given to us. It's truly a simple matter of attitudinal energy generated from within ourselves. Consistently thinking of needing more attracts that needy energy back to us. When we consistently generate thoughts of giving, however, we attract the energy of *giving back* to us.

Returning to Lao-tzu, he notes:

> *It is entirely possible for you to achieve immortality,*
> *and to experience absolute joy and freedom forever.*

*The practice of undiscriminating virtue
is the means to this end.*

*Practicing kindness and selflessness, you
naturally
align your life with the Integral Way.*[3]

The Shift is a contemporary interpretation of
this ancient teaching. I hope to impart to you
that Meaning is not achieved through your
ego and its selfish ways, but through the part
of yourself that is selfless. In the verse above,
Lao-tzu speaks of practicing "undiscriminating virtue"—this is your path to the freedom
and joy that characterize a purposeful life.

The Four Cardinal Virtues That
Constitute Our Original Nature

There is a book I love titled *Hua Hu Ching: The
Unknown Teachings of Lao Tzu,* by Brian Walker.
In these pages, Lao-tzu mentions four cardinal
virtues that are part of our original nature.
These virtues must be practiced if we are to

know the truth of our universe and achieve a life of Meaning while in bodily form.

While Brian Walker has done a masterful job in his book, I'd like to expand upon each of these virtues, one by one. Here they are, with a detailed explanation:

1. Reverence for all life. We begin life in this way, yet we then permit ego to engage us with complexity. Its demands pull the joy out of our days—always trying to get someplace or acquire more is an exhausting enterprise. Ultimately, desiring Meaning, we return to the place of our original nature. It seems that such a return must have prompted Voltaire to observe the following:

> One always begins with the simple, then comes the complex, and by superior enlightenment one often reverts in the end to the simple. Such is the course of human intelligence.[4]

When we return to our "Fromness," we're energized by a sense of wonder. The mysterious is welcomed rather than eschewed, and we find renewed pleasure in the simplest of activities. We no longer want others to be something they're not. In the Meaning phase of life, we remove the complexities that ego has foisted upon us, and the reverence we feel is often an intensely exhilarating sense of awe that we notice in nature. There's a newly experienced delight in hearing the wind howl, watching storms rage, and appreciating honeybees and butterflies do their job of pollinating the flowers.

The first cardinal virtue manifests itself as unconditional love and respect for ourselves and other beings. When we revere all of life, the desire to interfere, dominate, or control anyone is nonexistent. We adhere to these sweet words of the poet Robert Frost: "We love the things we love for what they are." When we practice this first cardinal virtue, we don't ask that people (or anything else, for that matter) live according to our expectations, which is what ego loves to do.

There are two ways to have the tallest building in town: One is ego's way, which is to knock the other buildings down until it has the tallest one. The problem with this method is that it creates constant conflict. People dislike when their accomplishments have been destroyed or diminished! Anger is the first response; followed by force, which is met with counterforce; and soon, all-out war is being waged. This is the way of ego—no reverence or love for others' accomplishments, only a need to compete and emerge victorious to proclaim superiority. In fact, ego is always on the lookout for someone with the temerity to try to top it.

The second way to have the tallest building in town is the way of Spirit, which offers Meaning over Ambition. This way urges us to put energy into our own building and respect others' efforts to do the same. There's no need to compete or triumph. There's no force, which always results in counterforce.

Reverence for all life involves love and respect for each of God's creatures, the planet, and the universe as well. When we practice this first cardinal virtue, we're at peace with the world and with ourselves. In the Meaning phase of life, we replace struggle with being ourselves—being lived by the great Tao.

2. Natural sincerity. The second cardinal virtue speaks to honesty in our daily lives. This doesn't necessarily mean that we'll refrain from breaking rules; rather, we're guided to enjoy an existence that is characterized by authenticity.

In the ego-driven Ambition phase, our false or inauthentic self is essentially in charge. That's when our idea of who we are is based on accumulating, achieving, gaining approval, and enhancing our separateness as an emblem of our superiority. It's impossible to be naturally sincere if we're attempting to be someone other than who we truly are, which is what happens when ego calls the shots.

As William Shakespeare puts it in *Hamlet:* "God has given you one face, and you make yourself another." When you alter your "face" to fit ego's image of who you are, you lose the ability to be naturally sincere. This quality results when you allow others to know you, without being afraid or worrying about how you're being perceived. Your speech and behavior basically send this message: *This is who I am. I came into this world with an inner calling to fulfill a destiny that will never be silenced.*

This provocative line, which is attributed to the children's author Dr. Seuss, underscores the meaning of the second cardinal virtue: "Be who you are and say what you feel, because those who mind don't matter, and those who matter don't mind." It's so true—those who matter won't mind your natural sincerity. Yet they will absolutely relish your fulfilling an inner sense of purpose and living a meaningful life. They want you to experience the joy of exploring becoming more of who you are, rather than striving to get someplace or become someone you really aren't.

I often speak with people who are sadly out of sync with their original nature. They describe unhappiness and frustration regarding their jobs, loathing the suits and ties they're required to wear, the hours they have to keep, and the people they work with. In general, these individuals are living from a very dishonest place, directed by factors that they believe define them. Of course, when asked if they're honest, they insist that they are. But the truth is that their lives are often devoid of Meaning, and they don't have a sense of fulfilling a dharma that they came here to actualize.

I always invite men and women who are in this situation to ponder this quote from Thoreau, which encourages natural sincerity: "If one advances confidently in the direction of his dreams, and endeavors to live the life which he has imagined, he will meet with a success unexpected in common hours."

Don't ask what the world needs; don't ask what others think you *should* be doing with your life. Instead, ask yourself what makes you come alive—because, more than anything else, what the world truly needs are men and women who have come alive. What the world needs is the natural sincerity of people living their passion in a way that makes other people's lives better. This is what being authentic looks like . . . and this, in my humble opinion, is what Lao-tzu meant when he called this second cardinal virtue of natural sincerity something that shows up as "honesty and a determination to be faithful to one's truest, most authentic self."

3. Gentleness. The third cardinal virtue for living from a position of Meaning points to kindness and consideration of others. As you know by now, this isn't ego's style. The false self is constantly on the prowl to exert power over others, since it feels separate. It's also threatened by the competitive nature of all of its relationships, and the need to exert force comes from that—and then, of course, the inevitable counterforce erupts when egos clash.

Our highest self doesn't feel threatened by others because it doesn't embrace the concept of separateness. Not feeling separate, our desire for a purposeful life nurtures a sense of unity with all other beings. This feeling of connectedness flows in the direction of compassion; ultimately, we reach out to the world with gentleness, humility, and kindness because we've returned to our original nature. In the words of Dr. Martin Luther King, Jr.:

"We are caught in an inescapable network of mutuality; tied in a single garment of destiny. Whatever affects one directly, affects all indirectly."

We won't experience Meaning as long as we're focused on violence. Thinking of conquering and vanquishing others, regardless of how compelling the reasons, prevents us from exercising the gentleness of our original nature. As the Tao Te Ching tells us:

Weapons are meant for destruction
and must be avoided by the wise.

Weapons aren't restricted to instruments of death; they're also the words and actions we use. Considering the importance of gentleness in living a meaningful life, we see how it leads us toward oneness. Both Lao-tzu and Jesus observed the constant warfare that existed between people and communities and admonished us to go with our highest nature if we desire Meaning and purpose in our lives.

How many people have perished because of man's inhumanity to man, which is the work of the false self? And for what? So many innocent beings in ancient villages have been slaughtered over who's going to rule the land, occupy the hilltop, or own the kingdom. A look at history reveals centuries of violence, with the 20th century being the most violent of all. And where are we today? Have we finally found a way to live together as one, as our highest nature implores us to do? We build weapons and store them in silos and submarines with the potential to terminate life on our planet for centuries to come. This absurdity results from so many of us acting exclusively on the directives of our egos.

We need to make the shift away from those perverse ego ambitions toward an existence that's more meaningful to all of us on planet Earth. If we make that shift and extend kindness and gentleness while eschewing violence, we'll feel the difference in our lifetime. We'll feel that we're finally home, thinking and acting like our Source of being. We'll feel true purpose. We'll feel the joyful authenticity of a life based on Meaning.

4. Supportiveness. The fourth cardinal virtue informs us that we are eternally supported in the process of living authentically. We let go of the Ambition imposed upon us by ego and relax into the Meaning that supports our particular life. Supportiveness manifests as service to others without expectation of reward or even a thank-you—it's the quintessential component of feeling that life has a purpose. It's the surest way to learn how to think like God thinks, which was Albert Einstein's primary motivation in attempting to unravel the mystery of creation. When we see ourselves as Divine, individualized expressions of God, we're more inclined to want to understand how the creative force operates.

What does God do with His hands? Does He ask for special treatment? Does He request help? Does He expect us to be grateful? Does He hoard things for Himself? Does He worry about how His work is judged? These are questions acquired from the false self, questions for which we create myths and stories to answer. Yet the true answer to these rhetorical questions is: *The only thing that God does with His hands is give, create, and offer over and over again. That's it.*

This fourth cardinal virtue tells us that our original nature—and the purpose of life—is like the sun. If we asked the sun why it always gives light, its answer would assuredly most likely be: "It's my nature to do so." The only thing we can do with life is give it away. Anything and everything else in the way of achievements or acquisitions mean nothing in the context of our purpose as spiritual beings having a human experience. We do not attract what we *want;* we attract what we *are.* The Prayer of St. Francis of Assisi makes clear that "it is in giving that we receive." Giving aligns us with the way our Source of being acts; consequently, the universe offers us experiences that match our giving, supportive nature.

Earlier, I described the way the universe responds back to us in the same vibrating energy that we send out. *How may I serve?* is the energy of support we send out—and receive in return. We see the beauty of this approach to life, not in the stuff we attract, but in a wondrous sense of contentment that replaces our ambitious, self-centered demands. We are living the Meaning of life.

Again turning to Shakespeare, I love this observation he makes in *Henry VI, Part III:*

My crown is in my heart, not on my head;
Not decked with diamonds and Indian stones,
Nor to be seen. My crown is called content:
A crown it is that seldom kings enjoy.

One of my personal heroes is Mother Teresa, who spent her later years teaching and serving others. She once remarked, "Love cannot remain by itself—it has no meaning. Love must be put into action, and that action is service." These words have inspired me and have helped me make the shift away from my ego's Ambitions for serving myself toward a life dominated by service to others.

Today my life is almost 100 percent devoted to service in one way or another. Each day begins with a prayer of "Thank you," which are the first words out of my mouth as I awaken. This is to keep me in a state of gratitude for all that I receive, as well as for the opportunity to live my days in service to others. As the famed Sufi poet Rumi once declared, "If you only say one prayer in a day, make it 'Thank you.'"

Before beginning my day, I make every effort to do something for someone else. Since I receive volumes of mail, I often send off a book or a DVD of *The Shift*, a set of CDs, or a DVD of a PBS special—something that I feel will brighten the day of a total stranger somewhere in the world. As I affix the postage, I take great joy in knowing that a surprise package of love in action will send a message to someone that there are people out there who care, and I am one of them.

Often I call someone I've been told is grieving the loss of a loved one or is ill in a hospital setting. Other times some money in an envelope goes to one of the many people who serve in my community. If I'm on the road in a hotel, I seek out the maids who serve me so anonymously and surprise them with a gift of some unexpected cash. The things I'm doing aren't reported for recognition, but to provide real-life examples of how shifting to Meaning affects daily life.

There are a multitude of ways in which we can give. It doesn't really matter what we do—the point is to get in the habit of replacing our attention on ourselves with attention toward others. We must practice some radical humility, seek out others to serve, keep ego at bay . . . and do it without expectation of any reward.

I'm much more of a minimalist than I was when my life was dominated by wishes and demands of my ego. I now take great pleasure in minimizing my accumulations. I frequently go through my closets, my library, and my personal acquisitions of all sorts and give things away with no expectation of a thank-you. I require very little in the way of luxuries; in fact, the less I have cluttering my living environment, the better I feel. As I stated previously, I don't let a single day go by without devoting myself to being supportive and in service to others. The irony is that the more I give away—and the more I spend time, energy, and money serving others—the more I get back. And it all keeps recycling, since without ego's attachment to my stuff and my earnings, the more I receive, and the more I'm able to give away.

Even so, I persistently remind myself of this fourth cardinal virtue because ego is tenacious and unwilling to retire gracefully. It pops up every now and again, urging me to think of myself first, to hoard what comes my way, and to expect huge thank-yous and elaborate expressions of gratitude for my being such a wonderful man. It tells me that I can't afford to support the people I do, or do things for others that my higher self wants to do.

Ego tells me, "You can't afford to be so generous, Wayne. You worked hard for what you have. You don't have to give the woman who is cleaning toilets in the hotel that much—just a dollar or two is sufficient. Back off and think of yourself first." On and on go these messages from ego. I sometimes find myself imagining putting my ego in a box, sealing it, and even sitting on it to keep it from resurfacing and pulling me away from my commitment to a life of meaning through practicing what I learned from Mother Teresa, which I'll reiterate: "Love must be put into action, and that action is service." I remind myself that love has no meaning if I let it remain alone and focused on me.

I'm reminded of Ram Dass, who told me that his years of putting his ego aside and being of service to his mother, father, and stepmother; as well as to people with AIDS and cancer, were the most fulfilling and meaningful times in his life. He'd carry his dad from his bed to the toilet, wipe and comfort him, never feeling that it was a burden. In fact, my friend called it the greatest opportunity of his life. Devoting himself to helping and being supportive allowed him to fully grasp the real meaning behind Lao-tzu's admonition to live this fourth cardinal virtue.

All of us can get into the habit of living a life based on service without expectation of reward by simply adopting a practice of radical humility. This is one of the key components of highly evolved people.

Just observe how nature operates: The ocean stays low yet gains tremendous strength. That's because all of the rivers and streams ultimately flow down and come to it. As the Tao Te Ching reminds us:

Why is the sea king of a hundred streams?
Because it lies below them.
Therefore, those desiring a position
above others must speak humbly.

Trees bend low with ripened fruit, clouds hang down with gentle rain, and noble leaders bow graciously. This is the way of Meaning and purpose. By practicing radical humility, we send a firm message to ego that we intend to have Meaning and purpose in our life and are going to live from these four cardinal virtues:

The four virtues are not an external dogma but a part of your original nature.
When practiced, they give birth to wisdom and evoke the five blessings: health, wealth, happiness, longevity, and peace.[5]

These traits describe people who have transcended their false selves and are living lives filled with Meaning. They are not tormented with questions like, *What if my whole life has been wrong?* They have made the shift to a higher level.

Shifting From Ambition To Meaning

There's a wonderful Turkish proverb that suc-
cinctly relates a message underlying *The Shift*.
It says: "No matter how far you have gone on a
wrong road, turn back." It doesn't matter how
long we've allowed ourselves to travel the road
of our false self. We know when it isn't leading
us to a sense of purpose and significance, and
we can admit we're on the wrong path. The
awareness that our life lacks Meaning is more
than enough evidence that it's time to make
a U-turn.

Here are three of the most important things
to watch out for as we shift to the path of a
meaningful and purposeful life:

1. The Shift from Entitlement to Humility

This is a monumental shift away from ego's
habitual thought pattern, which says that
we're *entitled* regardless of the impact on others or the planet. The fact is, we're entitled
to *nothing*. Nevertheless, ego's me-first self-

importance keeps us in a persistent state of frustration. This type of mentality provokes generalized anger at the world and many of the people in it.

A sense of entitlement is an irritating mind-set that creates friction. It appears uncaring, conceited, and only concerned with self. The directives we give to young, spoiled, ego-dominated children are valuable when we catch ourselves in ego's dominance. "Think of someone other than yourself," "Share your toys," and "Treat others the way you wish to be treated" and similar pieces of advice are good for us to follow, too, as we begin the shift From Ambition To Meaning. We must let go of the childish view that the world owes us. President John F. Kennedy's famous call to "ask not what your country can do for you—ask what you can do for your country," is a stirring reminder to collectively shift away from a sense of entitlement and in the direction of humility. Here, we're living from a place of God-realization rather than self-centeredness.

Making the shift to humility doesn't mean that we put ourselves down or are weak, but it does mean that we think of serving others before ourselves. Humility is the way of service, nurturing the sense of purpose that gives a dimension of significance to our lives. When we notice that we're thinking about what we're entitled to, we can remind ourselves that we're on the wrong road. Then we can find a way to return to humility and get back on track toward experiencing Meaning.

When we ask ourselves, "How can I want for someone else even more of what I'm feeling entitled to?" this may help suspend our sense of entitlement, if even for just a moment. Purpose blossoms through the practice of radical humility; it isn't nurtured in thoughts of what we feel we're entitled to.

2. The Shift from Control to Trust

If we're honest with ourselves, every one of us can agree that we're acquainted with the ego part that controls and manages our lives and eagerly attempts to do the same for others. Be they family, friends, co-workers, or even strangers, ego routinely accepts the job of edging God out and taking on the role of being the master manipulator. As we move in a different direction, we realize the pointlessness of attempting to control any individual or any situation. We recognize this need to practice interference as the power trip of our false self.

There was a time in my life, for instance, when I needed to be in charge of most social conversations. Having made the shift from control to trust means that I now flow with the conversational direction and opinions that are expressed. I'm content to sit back and observe, even as others take on the false-self role, as I view it. I can smile inwardly at some of my children's choices in life even when I disagree. The shift from control to trust has increased my noninterference.

Beyond my personal interactions with friends and family, in a much larger sense I trust more and control less. In my heart I know that God writes the books, delivers the speeches, and builds the bridges. When trust replaces control, edging God out isn't appealing. "All I have seen teaches me to trust the Creator for all I have not seen" may have been Ralph Waldo Emerson's words, but I agree so completely that they could be my own. I absolutely trust the wisdom of the universe and its creative Source.

With trust, we acknowledge our own wisdom. We remember that we came from the same Source and, therefore, must be like what we came from. We can trust Source to guide us, rather than screw things up with ego's demands for self-recognition and belief in our superiority. Trust lets us listen rather than take over. Listening allows us to comfortably sit back, knowing that the creative Source of everything is in charge instead of our puny little ego. Shifting from control to trust is so important for our life work.

In *The Shift* movie, I relate how I found the road that resonated with the calling of my soul. I did so by listening to what I was feeling deep within me, rather than what my ego was saying to me about how to capitalize on my fame by writing books to make more money. By trusting my inner excitement, I was able to make a big shift in my life, away from writing about psychology to writing about living life from a spiritual orientation. That shift away from the Ambition of ego, which tried to control my writing and speaking career, put me on the path of Meaning.

When *you* disengage from ego control, what is it that you trust? There are three markers to look for on this road. They are: trust in yourself, trust in others, and trust in the Source of being. Here's a brief explanation of each of them:

— **Trust in yourself.** This means hearing your soul speak in whatever way it does. Intuition is generally a reliable voice, in whatever form it expresses itself individually. Mahatma Gandhi explained his sense of it: "What is Truth? A difficult question; but I have solved it for myself by saying that it is what the 'voice within' tells you."

— **Trust in others.** This means noninterference as much as possible. Everyone has the universe located in him or her; trusting others frees you from feeling obligated to interfere. In the words of Lao-tzu in the Tao Te Ching:

Do you think you can take over the universe and improve it?
I do not believe it can be done.

Everything (and everyone) under heaven is a sacred vessel and cannot be controlled.
Trying to control leads to ruin.
Trying to grasp, we lose.

— **Trust in the Source of being.** This means trusting the mystery of creation. The universal Source of all creation, invisible though it may be, guides you just as it guided your development in the womb. When you trust in Divine intelligence, you cooperate and invite the shift to Meaning.

3. The Shift from Attachment to Letting Go

Perhaps the greatest lessons of my life have revolved around the slogan of the recovery moment: "Let go and let God"—a notion that involves relinquishing ego's attachment to, or fear of, something. The single most pronounced attachment for most of us during the morning of our lives is the attachment to being right! There's nothing ego loves more than to be right, which makes it an important and satisfying attachment to practice letting go of.

I seriously doubt that there's anyone reading this book who hasn't engaged in arguing about trivial matters that turned into disagreements, which had a net effect of following a road of self-righteous anger. And all of it probably seemed to be for no reason other than the need, the desire, to be *right!* Eventually we may look back with wistful amusement, realizing now that our fear of actually *being wrong* was so strong then that another person's opinion could energize this unwanted feeling. Ego's strategy was to be right no matter what, a highly successful maneuver that effectively distracted us from genuine purpose. Letting go of an attachment to being right is a fairly simple exercise.

The choice to let go and let God, in a quest to eliminate our attachment to being right, is simplified with these few words: *You're right about that.* But keep in mind that kindness and sincerity are necessary here, as opposed to sarcasm or insincerity. Those four words will gradually open the entry point to a road that leads through *letting go and letting God,* to experiencing more significance in life.

Another way to easily practice breaking ego's attachments is to clear out the garage, cupboards, and closets. Let go of material possessions, and practice not being attached to them. If they haven't been used in the past 12 months, they belong elsewhere. We can train ourselves to be one of "those" that Joel Goldsmith describes in his book *A Parenthesis in Eternity: Living the Mystical Life:*

> Then there are those who reach a stage in which they realize the futility of this constant striving and struggling for the things that perish, things which after they are obtained prove

to be shadows. It is at this stage that some persons turn from this seeking for things in the outer realm to a seeking for them from God.

Most stress results from hanging on to beliefs that keep us striving for more, because ego stubbornly refuses to believe we don't need something. When we make the shift, the influence of our ego fades. We replace attachment with contentment. Chasing and striving—and then becoming attached to what we chased after—is a source of anxiety that invigorates Ambition, but it won't satisfy the need for Meaning at our soul level. Everything that we pursue ultimately distances us from our original nature. All of our attachments are destined to perish. They are all shadows, as Goldsmith points out.

■ ■ ■

As we move in the direction of our authentic self, all of the shifts in this chapter on Meaning become natural ways of being. New attitudes feel good, and we notice how egoistic demands that we allowed to dominate our existence are no longer comfortable. Meaning has preeminence over ego's Ambition.

Living the four cardinal virtues and making the shifts to humility, trust, and letting go feel natural because we're rejoining our original nature. A life of Meaning is literally only a thought away.

I'm closing with Sir Laurens van der Post's words describing the African Bushmen's tale of two kinds of hunger and its relation to Meaning and purpose in our lives, which also opens the Introduction to this book. For me, these paragraphs are supremely symbolic on many levels. Reread them in the spirit of *The Shift*, knowing that each of us is responsible for the Meaning we find in our lives:

The Bushman in the Kalahari Desert talk about two "hungers."
There is the Great Hunger and there is the Little Hunger.
The Little Hunger wants food for the belly; but the Great Hunger,

the greatest hunger of all, is the hunger for
meaning. . . .

There's ultimately only one thing that makes
human beings deeply and profoundly bitter,
and that is to have thrust upon them
a life without meaning. . . .

There is nothing wrong in searching for
happiness. . . .
But of far more comfort to the soul . . .
is something greater than happiness
or unhappiness, and that is meaning.
Because meaning transfigures all. . . .
Once what you are doing has for you meaning,
it is irrelevant whether you're happy
or unhappy. You are content—you are not alone
in your Spirit—you belong.

(Sir Laurens van der Post from *Hasten Slowly,*
a film by Mickey Lemle)

ENDNOTES

Chapter One

1. From *The Prophet,* by Kahlil Gibran, published by Alfred A. Knopf, Inc.

2. From *Random House Webster's Quotationary,* by Leonard Frank, published by Random House.

3. From *Four Quartets,* by T. S. Eliot, published by Harcourt, Inc.

4. From *Quotationary.*

5. Ibid.

6. From *Treasury of Spiritual Wisdom: A Collection of 10,000 Powerful Quotations for Transforming Your Life,* by Andy Zubko, published by Motilal Banarsidass.

7. Ibid.

Chapter Two

1. From *Treasury of Spiritual Wisdom.*

2. From *Emmanuel's Book: A Manual for Living Comfortably in the Cosmos,* by Pat Rodegast and Judith Stanton, published by Bantam.

3. From *Treasury of Spiritual Wisdom.*

Chapter Three

1. From *The Portable Jung,* by Carl Jung and edited by Joseph Campbell, published by Viking Penguin Inc.

2. Quote reprinted with permission from the Elisabeth Kübler-Ross Foundation.

3. From *Rumi: Daylight,* translated by Camille and Kabir Helminski, published by Shambhala.

4. From *50 Self-Help Classics: 50 Inspirational Books to Transform Your Life,* by Tom Butler-Bowden, published by Nicholas Brealey Publishing.

Chapter Four

1. From *Hua Hu Ching: The Unknown Teachings of Lao Tzu,* by Brian Walker, published by HarperCollins.

2. Ibid.

3. Ibid.

4. From *Quotationary.*

5. From *Hua Hu Ching.*

— I thankfully acknowledge Mickey Lemle for permission to reprint from *Hasten Slowly: The Journey of Sir Laurens van der Post.* Please visit: **www.lemlepictures.com** for more information.

— Special thanks goes out to Leonard Frank, author of *Quotationary,* for putting together a masterful collection of quotes that has inspired me for years.

— Unless otherwise noted, quotations from the Tao Te Ching come from a public-domain version or from my own interpretation of this ancient sacred text, *Change Your Thoughts— Change Your Life.*

— Every attempt was made to credit all sources whenever applicable. Anyone with additional information is encouraged to contact: S. Littrell, Permissions Department, Hay House, Inc., P.O. Box 5100, Carlsbad, CA, 92018-5100. Any errors will be corrected on future reprints.

■   ■   ■   ■   ■

ABOUT THE AUTHOR

Dr. Wayne W. Dyer is an internationally renowned author and speaker in the field of self-development. He is the author of more than 30 books, has created many audio programs and videos, and has appeared on thousands of television and radio shows. His books *Manifest Your Destiny, Wisdom of the Ages, There's a Spiritual Solution to Every Problem,* and *The New York Times* bestsellers *10 Secrets for Success and Inner Peace, The Power of Intention, Inspiration, Change Your Thoughts—Change Your Life,* and *Excuses Begone!* have all been featured as National Public Television specials.

Wayne holds a doctorate in educational counseling from Wayne State University and was an associate professor at St. John's University in New York.

Website: **www.DrWayneDyer.com**

Hay House Titles of Related Interest

YOU CAN HEAL YOUR LIFE, the movie,
starring Louise L. Hay & Friends
(available as a 1-DVD program and
an expanded 2-DVD set)
Watch the trailer at: **www.LouiseHayMovie.com**

THE SHIFT, the movie,
starring Dr. Wayne W. Dyer
(available as a 1-DVD program and
an expanded 2-DVD set)
Watch the trailer at: **www.DyerMovie.com**

■ ■ ■

CHANTS OF A LIFETIME:
Searching for a Heart of Gold, by Krishna Das

A DAILY DOSE OF SANITY:
A Five-Minute Soul Recharge
for Every Day of the Year, by Alan Cohen

FROM STRESS TO SUCCESS . . . IN JUST 31 DAYS!
by Dr. John F. Demartini

GETTING PAST OK: The Self-Help Book
for People Who Don't Need Help, by Richard Brodie

THE GIFT OF FIRE:
How I Made Adversity Work for Me,
by Dan Caro, with Steve Erwin

POWER vs. FORCE: The Hidden Determinants of
Human Behavior, by David R. Hawkins, M.D., Ph.D.

SHIFT HAPPENS!
How to Live an Inspired Life Starting from Now,
by Robert Holden Ph.D.

SPONTANEOUS EVOLUTION:
Our Positive Future (and a Way to
Get There from Here),
by Bruce H. Lipton, Ph.D., and Steve Bhaerman

THE VORTEX: Where the <u>Law of Attraction</u> Assembles
All Cooperative Relationships, by Esther and Jerry Hicks
(The Teachings of Abraham®)

WHAT DOES THAT MEAN? Exploring Mind, Meaning,
and Mysteries, by Eldon Taylor

■ ■ ■

All of the above are available at your local bookstore,
or may be ordered by contacting Hay House.

NOTES

NOTES

NOTES

NOTES

NOTES

NOTES

NOTES

NOTES

NOTES

NOTES

NOTES

JOIN THE HAY HOUSE FAMILY

As the leading self-help, mind, body and spirit publisher in the UK, we'd like to welcome you to our family so that you can enjoy all the benefits our website has to offer.

 EXTRACTS from a selection of your favourite author titles

 COMPETITIONS, PRIZES & SPECIAL OFFERS Win extracts, money off, downloads and so much more

 LISTEN to a range of radio interviews and our latest audio publications

 CELEBRATE YOUR BIRTHDAY An inspiring gift will be sent your way

 LATEST NEWS Keep up with the latest news from and about our authors

 ATTEND OUR AUTHOR EVENTS Be the first to hear about our author events

 iPHONE APPS Download your favourite app for your iPhone

 HAY HOUSE INFORMATION Ask us anything, all enquiries answered

join us online at **www.hayhouse.co.uk**

 292B Kensal Road, London W10 5BE
T: 020 8962 1230 E: info@hayhouse.co.uk

We hope you enjoyed this Hay House book.
If you would like to receive a free catalogue featuring additional
Hay House books and products, or if you would like information
about the Hay Foundation, please contact:

Hay House UK Ltd
292B Kensal Road • London W10 5BE
Tel: (44) 20 8962 1230; Fax: (44) 20 8962 1239
www.hayhouse.co.uk

***

Published and distributed in the United States of America by:
Hay House, Inc. • PO Box 5100 • Carlsbad, CA 92018-5100
Tel: (1) 760 431 7695 or (1) 800 654 5126;
Fax: (1) 760 431 6948 or (1) 800 650 5115
www.hayhouse.com

***

Published and distributed in Australia by:
Hay House Australia Ltd • 18/36 Ralph Street • Alexandria, NSW 2015
Tel: (61) 2 9669 4299, Fax: (61) 2 9669 4144
www.hayhouse.com.au

***

Published and distributed in the Republic of South Africa by:
Hay House SA (Pty) Ltd • PO Box 990 • Witkoppen 2068
Tel/Fax: (27) 11 467 8904
www.hayhouse.co.za

***

Published and distributed in India by:
Hay House Publishers India • Muskaan Complex • Plot No.3
B-2• Vasant Kunj • New Delhi - 110 070
Tel: (91) 11 41761620; Fax: (91) 11 41761630
www.hayhouse.co.in

***

Distributed in Canada by:
Raincoast • 9050 Shaughnessy St • Vancouver, BC V6P 6E5
Tel: (1) 604 323 7100
Fax: (1) 604 323 2600

***

Sign up via the Hay House UK website to receive the Hay House
online newsletter and stay informed about what's going on with your
favourite authors. You'll receive bimonthly announcements
about discounts and offers, special events, product highlights,
free excerpts, giveaways, and more!
www.hayhouse.co.uk